Everything You Ever
Wanted to Ask About ...
Periods

Fiona Finlay has worked as a Community Paediatrician in Bath, Bristol and Southampton. She is currently a Community Paediatric Consultant in Bath, where she lives with her two young children. Her professional interests include child protection and adolescent medicine. This is her first book for Piccadilly Press.

Rosemary Jones qualified as a doctor in Leeds twenty-two years ago. She currently works as a Consultant Paediatrician in Bath. Her professional interests include management of children with autism, the care of children who are fostered and adopted, and adolescent medicine. This is her first book for Piccadilly Press.

Tricia Kreitman worked as a psychologist, designing sex education programmes for young people, and then as a psychosexual therapist before becoming a full-time author and broadcaster. She has been an Agony Aunt for 15 years, working on the teenage magazine *Mizz* and the women's monthly, *Prima*. A parent of teenagers herself, Tricia was Vice-Chair of Brook Advisory Centres for young people for five years. She is an experienced TV and radio broadcaster and was co-presenter of "You TV" and "Living and Growing", videos frequently used in school PHSE programmes. She has written three books for young people. This is her first book for Piccadilly Press.

Everything You Ever Wanted to Ask About ...
Periods

Tricia Kreitman, Fiona Finlay & Rosemary Jones

Piccadilly Press • London

To all our families

First published in Great Britain in 2001
by Piccadilly Press Ltd.,
5 Castle Road, London NW1 8PR

A catalogue record for this book is available from
the British Library

ISBNs: 1 85340 672 4 (trade paperback)

9 10 8

Printed and bound in Great Britain
by Bookmarque Ltd.

Cover design by Paul Fielding Design, Ltd.
Design by Louise Millar
Set in 11pt Myriad

Contents

Acknowledgements

We would like to thank all the girls who helped us with this book by talking to us, confiding their problems, answering our questions and telling us what they really wanted to know.

We are particularly grateful to all the *Mizz* readers who helped us and to Emily, Alice and Polly Jones for all their advice.

How to Use This Book

- Everything in this book is based on what real girls have said they really want to know.
- You may choose to read straight through from the beginning to the end, or just pick out the sections that sound most interesting to you.
- Apart from Chapter One, each chapter begins with a list of the topics covered in that section.
- Most chapters also have true-life stories and problem pages.
- Finally, because it's so hard to talk about your bodies and what's happening inside you without using some medical or technical names, we've made a list (glossary) with all the words you might not know. These words usually show up in *italics* and you can look them up in the glossary at the back of the book where it explains what they mean.

Introduction

In the 15 years that I have been the Agony Aunt for the UK teenage magazine *Mizz*, I've probably received something like 200,000 letters (yes, the letters on problem pages really *are* genuine) from girls aged ten to seventeen. Amongst the problems with boyfriends, worries about weight and complaints about over-protective parents, there has been a constant stream of letters about periods. In fact, in any post-bag about 20% of letters would probably be connected with periods and puberty.

The questions that girls ask include:
- *How will I know when I'm about to start my periods?*
- *Exactly how much blood do you lose?*
- *If you carry on bleeding for several days, how come you don't bleed to death?*
- *If you wear a tampon, what happens when you go to the loo?*
- *Does blood leak out when you are in water?*
- *What do you do if it starts and you haven't got anything with you?*
- *Will other people be able to tell that you're having your period?*
- *Will it really, really hurt?*

Reading all these letters made me realise just how many girls were still worried and confused about something that happens – and has always happened – to all women. Three things were particularly clear:
- Lessons in school about periods and growing up often tell girls too little, too late.
- Many parents find it difficult or even impossible to talk about periods and body changes.

- The information that parents or schools do give is often biological rather than practical. As one girl put it: "They just showed us diagrams and talked about hormones. What we really wanted to know was what to do if your period suddenly started when you weren't expecting it."

In 1995 I was lucky enough to meet two consultant paediatricians (doctors specialising in children and young people's medicine), Fiona Finlay and Rosemary Jones. They were working with young people in schools and clinics and had been hearing the same questions that girls were writing to me at *Mizz*. They shared my concerns and together we started to look more closely at the problem.

We have been researching what happens – and when – to girls as they grow up. We have published results and spoken at conferences for many professionals working in health and education, but our main aim was to help the girls themselves. We wanted to get rid of the misunderstandings, confusion and worries surrounding periods so we decided to write this book.

We didn't write it for professionals or parents – although they may be interested to see what's in it! This book was especially written for girls who are about to start or have already started their periods. Hopefully, this will give them the answers to some of their worries, or at least the confidence to ask for more help and advice if they need it. Everything we have written is in direct response to what young people have asked us or told us they wished they had known, and every section has lots of quotes from girls talking about their own experiences.

TRICIA KREITMAN

CHAPTER 1

Why Do I Need to Know All This?

Periods are a natural part of growing up and becoming a woman, so you might wonder what all the fuss is about! We wrote this book because so many girls had asked us for advice and information about periods. You might also find it useful for the following reasons:

- *Because even if your periods haven't started yet, one day they will.* You can then probably expect to have one every month for about 40 years. The average period lasts for about five days each month, so if you added all those days together you could calculate that about six and a half years of your life will be spent having periods! It makes sense to find out as much as possible about periods so you're really well prepared.

- *Because many people (parents included) find it difficult to talk openly about periods.* Advertisements for pads and tampons add to this embarrassment by never mentioning the word "blood" and using blue-coloured liquid instead of red when they show how absorbent their products are. They also give the impression that it would be the most embarrassing thing in the world if someone discovered you were having your period. So it's not surprising that lots of women go to great lengths to hide the fact that they're having them, even from their own families. Unfortunately this becomes a vicious circle and a girl can easily pick up this feeling of embarrassment from her mum, making it hard for her to ask questions and just as difficult to talk to her own daughter about periods when the time comes.

- **Because although you'll probably have lessons about periods at school, these may concentrate more on biology than practical advice.** Understanding what's going on inside your body is very important, but most girls worry far more about what a period will really feel like and exactly what they need to do to cope. It's these questions that are often left unanswered.

- **Because you may hear myths and rumours, so it's important to know the truth.** Probably because periods are still such an embarrassing topic for so many people, there are lots of misunderstandings around. For example, you might hear that it's dangerous to have a bath or to do any strenuous exercise during your period. In fact the opposite is true. Regular baths or showers are important to help you feel clean and comfortable and, although you may feel a bit tired before and during the first few days of your period, exercise is a very good way of easing period pains and making yourself feel better. Once you learn more about periods and read the problem pages in this book (which are all based on real questions from real girls) you'll be able to sort out fact from fiction.

- **Because although periods are normal, it's also normal to have worries or questions.** Starting your periods can seem a big step (though it's important to remember that you're still the same person you were before) and it's only natural to have some questions. And sometimes, even when you've been having periods for ages, things can happen that you may not be too sure about or would like some advice on. Hopefully this book will answer a lot of these questions – or give you the confidence to ask for further help if you need it.

- **Because so many girls suffer from peer pressure about their bodies, it's important to understand that everyone is different.** People start puberty at different times and, even then, some grow quickly and others more slowly. Many girls feel worried and left out because their bodies are "different" in some way. Knowing that it's OK not to be the same as your friends can help you to stop worrying.

- **Because your friends might not be as clued up as you, so you can help them out.** You aren't the only one this is happening to. And some girls find it very hard to share their fears and worries. Once you've read this book you'll be in a very good position to help your friends to cope by answering all those difficult questions that nobody else seems quite sure about.

- **Because you're going to have lots of advertising aimed at you.** The people who make sanitary products like pads and tampons know they're on to a good thing. If they can get you using their product, there's a chance you'll carry on buying the same brand month after month for years on end. So they're going to spend a lot of money to persuade you that theirs is best. Perhaps it is very good, but no single product is best for everyone.

Many girls use a mixture of different things according to how heavy their periods are. And what works for your friend might not be so comfortable or suitable for you. Understanding how different products work and knowing that it's fine to chop and change can help you see through some of the advertising hype and make decisions for yourself.

And ... finally:

- **Because thousands of girls have told us that these are the things they really wanted to know.**

CHAPTER 2

Periods and Puberty – Basic Biology

This chapter explains:
- **What Puberty Is**
- **How Your Body Changes**
- **What's Going On Inside You**
- **What Happens Every Month**
- **What Happens to Boys**
- **Making Love – and Babies**

This chapter explains how your body works and what's happening inside you when you have a period. You may already know some – or even a lot – of this from school or other books, or you may be put off by the idea of diagrams and difficult words that look like a science lesson! You don't have to read this chapter now if you don't feel like it – but you may want to come back to it later.

What Puberty Is

Puberty is the word that describes all the changes that take place as you grow and change from being a child into an adult. Having your first period is just one stage of puberty.

How Your Body Changes

A girl's body changes from
something like this:

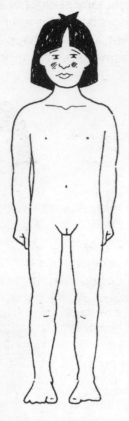

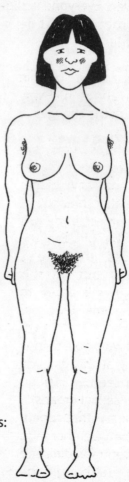

to something more like this:

Puberty starts with a few pubic hairs and budding breasts and ends with you being able to have children. So it's quite a change!

Everyone goes through puberty – but it can start at different times. Half of all girls will have noticed the first changes by the time they are ten but it could be as early as eight or as late as 14 or 15. It can last a couple of years or take as long as six or seven. Everyone is slightly different, and what happens to you probably won't be exactly the same as what happens to your friends.

This is a picture of a girl who's about half-way through the changes of puberty.

Perhaps you are taller or shorter, fatter or thinner, have bigger or smaller breasts, or more or less body hair than this girl. But the changes that we've pointed out on this picture will apply to you at some stage too.

If you were able to look closely at this girl, you could see her genitals (outer sexual organs).

She has three openings between her legs, the urethra, vagina and anus – although the

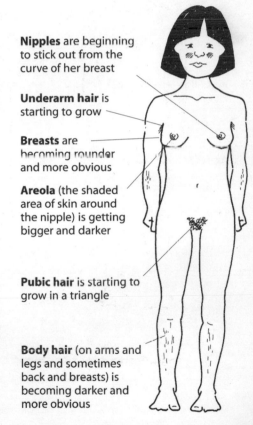

Nipples are beginning to stick out from the curve of her breast

Underarm hair is starting to grow

Breasts are becoming rounder and more obvious

Areola (the shaded area of skin around the nipple) is getting bigger and darker

Pubic hair is starting to grow in a triangle

Body hair (on arms and legs and sometimes back and breasts) is becoming darker and more obvious

17

opening of the urethra is so small it can be difficult to see. Stools (poo, number twos) are passed out through her anus and urine (pee, wee or water) comes out of the urethra. The vagina is the opening where blood from a period flows out, and it is also the sex passage where a penis is inserted during love-making, and the birth canal through which babies are born.

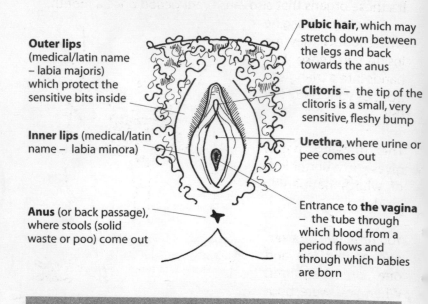

Outer lips (medical/latin name – labia majoris) which protect the sensitive bits inside

Inner lips (medical/latin name – labia minora)

Anus (or back passage), where stools (solid waste or poo) come out

Pubic hair, which may stretch down between the legs and back towards the anus

Clitoris – the tip of the clitoris is a small, very sensitive, fleshy bump

Urethra, where urine or pee comes out

Entrance to **the vagina** – the tube through which blood from a period flows and through which babies are born

Perhaps it's never occurred to you to have a look between your legs – or maybe you've heard or thought that it would be dirty or wrong. This isn't true. If you do want to get to know your own body better, take a look at it using a small mirror. Don't worry if you don't look exactly like the picture above – everyone is slightly different!

What's Going On Inside You

Some of the most important changes that occur during puberty take place **inside** your body where you can't see them. They involve your *reproductive organs*. These are the parts of the body that produce eggs and allow a baby to form and develop. It's these organs that also cause your period once a month.

To help you imagine whereabouts they are inside you, make your hands into a triangle in front of your body like this:

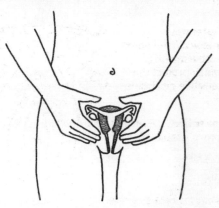

The drawing below gives you a better idea of what's happening inside you.

You have two **ovaries**, one on the left and one on the right. When you were born there were already thousands and thousands of very tiny eggs inside each ovary. When you reach puberty one or two of these eggs are released each month.

The ovaries are also

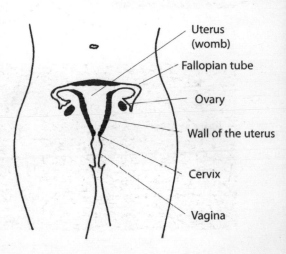

Uterus (womb)

Fallopian tube

Ovary

Wall of the uterus

Cervix

Vagina

19

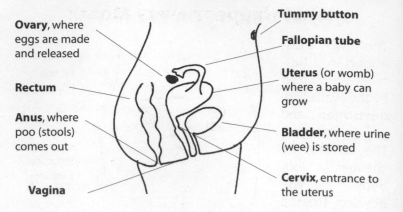

Ovary, where eggs are made and released

Tummy button

Fallopian tube

Rectum

Uterus (or womb) where a baby can grow

Anus, where poo (stools) comes out

Bladder, where urine (wee) is stored

Vagina

Cervix, entrance to the uterus

very important because they produce **hormones** that control the **cycle** or pattern of your periods.

You've probably heard people talking about hormones. They are natural chemicals that your body produces to help control just about everything – but particularly how you grow and change.

What is a Hormone?

Hormones are like chemical messengers. They are made in one part of the body (usually in a gland) and then, using the blood stream as a transport system, they travel all over the place delivering instructions. This doesn't just happen during puberty. You were producing hormones before you were even born and you'll go on producing them all through your life.

What Happens Every Month

The two most important hormones produced by the ovaries are **oestrogen** and **progesterone**. They cause the changes in your body as you develop from a girl to a woman, and they control the monthly cycle of your periods.

Hormones tell the ovaries when to release an egg. Once an egg is released, it moves slowly along the Fallopian tube to the uterus.

Although the Fallopian tubes are only about 10–12 cm long, it can take an egg up to a week to travel the full distance. Around the time the egg

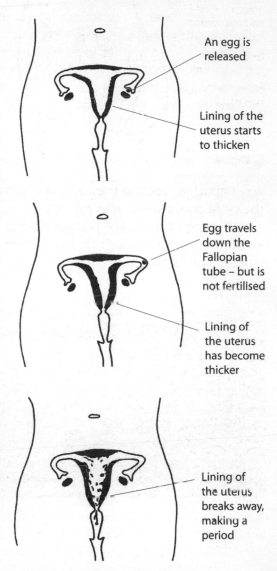

An egg is released

Lining of the uterus starts to thicken

Egg travels down the Fallopian tube – but is not fertilised

Lining of the uterus has become thicker

Lining of the uterus breaks away, making a period

is released, the lining of the uterus starts to become thicker.

If the egg met a sperm during its journey down the Fallopian tube it might become fertilised. This is when an egg and a sperm join together then start to grow by producing more and more cells. The group of cells then moves down the Fallopian tube and into the uterus. If it nestles into the wall of the **uterus** it can grow into a tiny foetus and eventually a baby.

However, if the egg gets all the way to the uterus without being fertilised by a sperm, it starts to break up. At the same time, the lining of the uterus begins to break away into little pieces, as it is not needed to nourish (or feed) a foetus. It forms an oozy mixture of blood, dead cells and the microscopic egg, that slowly flows out of the body through the vagina. This is what makes a period.

What Happens to Boys

Boys go through puberty too! It tends to start a bit later than in girls, and like girls, everyone is different.

Girls usually have their main growth spurt early in puberty, before they start their periods, but boys may not start their growth spurt until they are 13 or 14, and they often carry on growing all the way through puberty. This explains why many 11- and 12-year-old girls are taller than boys of the same age.

As well as growing taller, boys' shoulders and chests tend to become wider. They get lots of body hair, which often starts under their arms and around their penis, but spreads all over their body, and also of course, their face. Some have to start shaving early while others may not need to shave until much later. Boys' voices also get deeper. Sometimes this happens

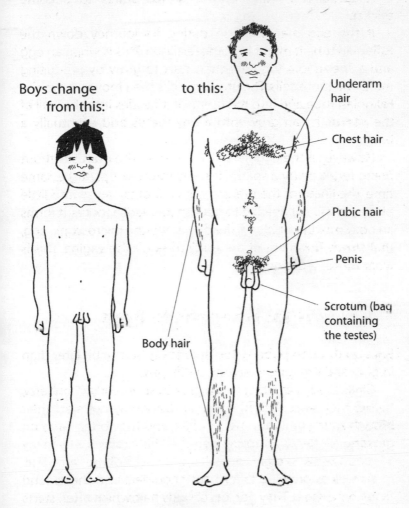

Boys change from this: to this:

Underarm hair

Chest hair

Pubic hair

Penis

Scrotum (bag containing the testes)

Body hair

suddenly or it can take place gradually. When this happens, people say that a boy's voice has "broken".

There's a big change in boys' sexual organs too. Their *penis* and *testes* get bigger.

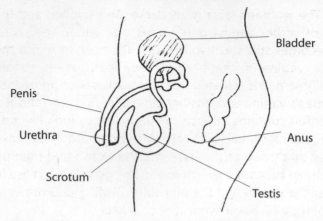

The testes (plural of testis) are soft balls about the size of small plums that hang behind the penis in the *scrotum*, a loose bag of skin. The testes make hormones which control growth and development in different parts of the body. The testes also produce sperm, the male sex cells which can fertilise a girl's egg to make a baby.

The penis is made of spongy tissue with a small tube, the *urethra*, running through it. Just like a girl, a boy passes urine (pee) through his urethra. This is also the tube that sperm comes out of – though not at the same time as urine!

When a boy becomes sexually excited, his penis grows swollen and stiff. Eventually, a small amount of white, cloudy liquid may spurt out of the end of it. This is called *semen* and is a mixture of sperm and fluid.

Making Love – and Babies

When two people make love (have sex) they usually start off by touching and kissing each other. This feels very good and they both begin to get a pleasant warm feeling in their sexual organs. The woman's labia grow darker and swollen and the inner part of her vagina gets longer and wider. The man's penis becomes stiff and swollen so that he can fit it into the woman's vagina if that's what they both want to do. Eventually semen is released from his penis, shooting up into the woman's vagina towards her cervix. This semen (about a teaspoonful) contains millions of sperm – they look like tiny tadpoles with long tails and can swim very hard. They make their way up through the cervix, into the womb and then up the Fallopian tubes. If a sperm meets an egg it can fertilise it. Together the sperm and the egg start dividing and growing into a foetus which will eventually be a baby.

Amazing Facts

- A human egg is so tiny that you could fit ten of them into the space of one full stop!
- Girls are born with over a million eggs in their ovaries but, in their whole life, only about 400 will ever be released.
- The inside of a Fallopian tube is about the same width as a human hair. It is delicate and can easily be damaged or blocked. One reason why it is important to guard against infections in your sexual organs is that blocked Fallopian tubes can stop you becoming pregnant when you're older.
- During pregnancy, as the baby grows, the uterus gets over 1,000 times bigger than usual!
- A sperm is only 0.05 mm long – 200 sperm laid end to end would only be 1 cm long.
- A sperm can swim about 3 mm an hour, or about 7 cm in 24 hours.
- Approximately 500,000,000 sperm are made every day by a healthy adult man.

Problem Page

I looked between my legs with a mirror but I can only see two holes – my vagina and back passage. Is there something wrong with me?
No, it's just that the third hole, the opening of your urethra, is very tiny and sometimes difficult to see. But it's where your urine comes out and it will be there somewhere!

When I looked between my legs my inner lips were much bigger than my outer lips. Is there something wrong with me?
No, although on diagrams the inner lips are usually shown as being smaller, they are often larger or hang down lower than the outer lips. And sometimes one side is larger than the other. It's nothing to worry about. You are quite normal!

I have an illness called coeliac disease which means I can't eat anything with wheat in it. I was very poorly until I was about five and, although I'm better now, I'm a lot smaller than my friends. Will I ever grow up like them? Do girls like me have periods?
All sorts of long-term conditions can affect how you grow. On the whole, taller girls start their periods earlier than smaller girls (though there are some exceptions). There's no medical reason why your periods shouldn't start, but they may come a bit later than everyone else's. If you're worried about this you could ask your doctor or school nurse for more advice.

Is there anything I can do to make my periods start? All my friends have got theirs and I feel like a baby.
No, there really isn't anything you can do to make your periods come any earlier. The age and rate at which you will develop is already programmed into your body. However it is worth considering whether you are the right sort of weight

for your height. Ask your school nurse or GP if you aren't sure. Periods can be delayed in girls who are underweight.

I've heard that you stop growing once your periods start. Is this true?
Not exactly. You'll do most of your growing before your periods start, and you may notice a growth spurt in the year or so before your first period. Once your periods begin, growth slows down but you will probably get a little bit taller over the next few years. You'll probably notice that your feet stop growing first!

CHAPTER 3

When Will My Periods Start?

This chapter covers:
- **Average Age for Starting Periods**
- **Changes You May Notice Before Your First Period Starts**
- **The Growth Spurt**
- **Breasts, Pubic Hair, Spots, Smells and Discharge**
- **Hormones and Emotions**

Average Age for Starting Periods

Although the whole process of *puberty* can take several years, and you may not even notice some of it happening, starting your first period is a very special event. The medical term for it is *menarche*. Most girls begin their periods between the ages of 12 and 13 – but lots start earlier or later. Some start their periods when they're only eight or nine, others don't begin until they're 16 or 17. Many girls worry when their body doesn't do the "average" thing, so it's important to understand that everyone is different.

I started my periods when I was 9 and I was lucky as my mum had realised what was happening and explained it to me in time. It was still hard because I was bigger than everyone at school and it was obvious my boobs were starting to grow. I got teased a lot and I was really scared they'd find out about my periods.

Alice, 12

All my friends seemed to start their periods when they were 12 or 13 and I felt really left out. Everyone talked about it so it was easier to pretend I was having them too. I even took to carrying pads around with me in my school bag. Then my mum found them and asked why I hadn't told her that I'd started. I didn't know what to say but eventually it all came out and she told me that she hadn't started until she was 15. I am quite small like her so now I'm not so worried. Though I haven't told my friends that I was making it up!

Lucy, 14

When I reached 16 and still hadn't started, I was sure there had to be something wrong with me. My mum kept asking me if there was anything I wanted to talk about but I was too scared to say anything. All my friends thought I'd started and I just used to keep quiet when they talked about periods. Then, one day, I was at the doctor's with earache and she asked me if I'd started yet. I nearly died! But she was so nice and told me about all the signs that come beforehand. She said that although I was late getting my period she thought I'd start soon. I was so relieved! Then, about two weeks later, I noticed dark brown spots on my pants and I realised it was finally starting.

Gail, 17

When you're talking to your mum about periods, it's a good idea to ask her how old she was when she started. Many girls start at around the same time as their mum or their older sister.

Changes You May Notice Before Your First Period Starts

Your period isn't the only thing that happens to your body during puberty. Other changes can appear up to two years before your first period. If you're waiting for your periods to start, these changes will let you know that they are on their way.

The Growth Spurt

This is when your body puts a lot of energy into growing – usually upwards but sometimes outwards too. Babies have a growth spurt for the first two years of their life. After that most girls grow at about 5 cm a year until just before they start puberty. Then there's another growth spurt where everything speeds up and they may grow twice as much in one year as before.

Soon after you've had your first period your growth will slow down again.

Breasts, Pubic Hair, Spots, Smells and Discharge

Breast changes
When your breasts start to develop, this is one very obvious sign of puberty.

Breasts are made up from fat and a special sort of spongy tissue which has tiny glands in it. If you have a baby the glands can produce milk to feed it.

One of the first signs of puberty may be when you start to develop *breast buds*. These are small, hard lumps about the size of a grape behind each nipple. They may feel a bit tender. Next, the coloured area around the nipple (the *areola*) starts to widen, darken and become more obvious. Your breasts continue to grow until they get to their full grown-up shape and size – but this may take several years.

The diagrams below show you what happens.

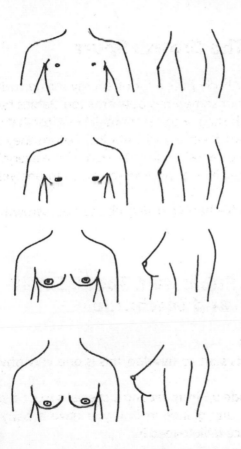

Breasts buds are developing

Areola becomes more obvious and breasts get bigger

Full-grown breasts

Other changes in your body

Your shape usually changes as you start puberty. Most girls find that their hips get a little wider or rounder and their feet get bigger.

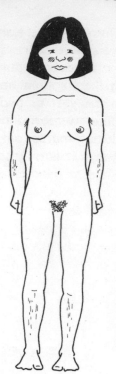

You'll find your first *pubic* hairs growing between your legs, and a few hairs in your armpits too. As puberty continues, you get gradually hairier. You will notice more hairs on your legs and arms and possibly a few on your lower back – or even your breasts. Your pubic hair will become thicker and curlier, spreading up a little and maybe even down a bit on to your upper thighs and between your legs towards your bottom.

Spots, smells and discharge

There are also some less welcome signs of puberty. The oil glands in your skin become more active, often leading to spots and acne. Taking care to keep your face clean and using special oil control washes and products can help, but you can always ask the chemist or your GP for advice too. Doctors can prescribe some very effective medicines for acne.

Sweat glands become more active; not just those under your arms but also those on the soles of your feet, the palms of your hands and even between your legs. It can be a big problem if you let the sweat get stale and smelly. Having a daily shower or bath and wearing clean clothes will help, but you may also want to start using a deodorant or anti-perspirant. A deodorant covers up the smell whereas an antiperspirant cuts down the amount of sweat produced. Lots of products contain both.

In the year or two before your periods start, you may become aware of damp stains in your pants. Your cervix is producing *mucus* (oozy liquid) which comes out as *vaginal discharge*. It is quite normal – and a kind of self-cleaning mechanism. The discharge carries out with it any dead cells or dirt. It may be clear or milky-white coloured, drying to a creamy, flaky paste on your pants. It has a natural smell that may be slightly yeasty or biscuity. As you get closer to starting your periods, this discharge can become quite heavy. When your periods do start the normal discharge mixes with the blood, so it may look as though you're bleeding a lot more than you really are.

Hormones and Emotions

It's not just your body that changes during puberty. Your emotions are affected too! The hormones that cause you to grow and change can have an effect on your mood as well. You are you – and nothing is ever going to change that, but you don't always feel the same inside. Sometimes you are happy and other times you may feel a bit sad or down. Often there's a reason for this. You might have had a row with a friend or got a bad mark at school. There may be occasions when something little happens to annoy you, and you simply can't cope. You may find it impossible to watch sad films or unpleasant news items without sobbing your heart out. Or perhaps you wake up one morning when there's really nothing to worry about – but you still feel miserable or tearful.

These feelings can be frightening, particularly if the people around you appear unsympathetic. Luckily they usually pass quite quickly and you bounce back to the "normal" you.

Here's a list of some things you can do to help shake off these moods:

- Get out into the fresh air and (if possible) sunlight. Even a ten-minute brisk walk will help lift your mood.
- Listen to some music you enjoy – something you can sing or dance to is particularly good.
- If you're feeling really angry shut yourself in your bedroom and beat up your pillow.
- Talk to someone who understands – your mum or a best friend.
- Write down your feelings as a diary, a story or a poem. You don't ever have to show it to anyone if you don't want to, but sometimes putting feelings down on paper helps.

I was about 11 when I started feeling really miserable for no obvious reason. Sometimes I'd be fine then someone would say something and I'd fly off the handle, then burst into tears. I didn't know why I was doing it and it didn't help when my mum said how difficult I was being.

Sally, 14

I used to get really embarrassed watching telly with my family. If there was someone kissing or the slightest suggestion of soppy stuff I'd go all peculiar and start blushing. I felt that everyone was looking at me all the time. It was even worse if we were watching something sad or even if I just listened to a sad song on the radio. I'd cry very easily and my brothers used to tease me.

Kaz, 15

My daughter Suzie started her periods at 13 but we knew they were on the way because she was so difficult for a whole year beforehand. We felt we were walking on eggshells the whole time and you never knew whether she'd be her normal, sunny self or start screaming about how unfair we all were. Even worse were the days when she didn't want to come out of her room and you could tell she'd been crying. I was so worried about her but she wouldn't talk to me. Finally my sister (Suzie's aunt) was staying and Suzie opened up to her, saying how scared she got with her moods. My sister was able to explain that most women feel like this sometimes and that it didn't stop any of us loving her. Since then things have been a lot easier!

Suzie's mum

Problem Page

I've found a lump under one of my nipples. It's about as big as a grape but it hurts when I squeeze it. I'm really scared. What is it? Could it be cancer?

It's very, very, very rare for young girls to get breast cancer. What you can feel sounds like a normal breast bud. These are small hard lumps just behind your nipples and they are one of the first signs that your body is starting to develop. Often one breast begins to grow before the other. However if you're really worried, it is always a good idea to get a doctor to check it out.

I'm 12 years old and one of my boobs is quite a lot bigger than the other. What's wrong with me?

Don't worry – there's nothing wrong. Many girls find that their boobs get a bit lopsided – especially while they're still growing. However most women end up with breasts which are more or less the same size.

All my friends have been wearing bras for ages, but I haven't got one. It's horrid when I get changed for games as they all make fun of me because I don't wear one. How can I get my mum to understand that I need to wear a bra?

Maybe your mum is waiting for you to raise the subject? She may not want to suggest buying you bras before she's sure you're ready, but if she knew how embarrassed you felt at school, I think she'd help you to find some nice bras or crop tops that you could wear. Your breasts may not be big enough yet to really need the support but if you feel embarrassed not wearing one, then that's a good enough reason to start.

My breasts are much flatter than everyone else's. How can I make them bigger?

Your basic body shape is inherited from your parents. If your mum is fairly flat-chested (or was as a girl) then you probably will be too. Some girls find that their breasts develop quickly but with others it's a slow process that takes many years. There's nothing you can do to make them grow faster, but standing up straight with your shoulders back and wearing a comfortable but supportive bra will help make the most of what you have.

My breasts have grown much bigger very suddenly. They're uncomfortable when I run and play sport and the boys at school keep teasing me. Is there anything I can do?

Maybe you're the first to start developing, so people notice and that's why you feel self-conscious or embarrassed. It's very important to wear a bra that fits properly, so ask your mum to take you to a shop where you can be measured and helped to choose one that's comfortable and gives you the support you need. It's also worth getting a special sports bra which helps prevent the uncomfortable jiggling when you run. Try to ignore the teasing as much as possible – but make sure you have someone sympathetic to talk to about it, e.g. your mum or PE teacher.

My hair is light brown, but the pubic hair between my legs looks quite red. Am I abnormal?
Pubic hair is not always exactly the same colour as the hair on your head so there's nothing to worry about.

I've got these awful red lines on my breasts and at the top of my thighs. I asked my mum about them and she said they were stretch marks. She had them when she was pregnant. But I'm only 12! What's going on?
I suspect your body has been changing quite a lot in the last few months. As you've gone through puberty, your breasts have been getting bigger and your hips and legs more rounded. This is normal and shows that you are changing from a girl to a woman. Sometimes it happens so fast that the skin becomes stretched, leaving these bright red marks. Some people seem to get them really easily, but the stretch marks you get during puberty usually fade. Keeping your skin well moisturised with baby lotion or E45 cream will help.

I'm 13 and have cerebral palsy so I have to use a wheelchair. I have a helper at school and I manage most things well but I do have a problem. No one seems to realise that I'm growing up and although lots of my friends have started their periods no one has said anything to me about them. My mum is really great but she's very protective and thinks I'm still a child.
Being in a wheelchair won't affect your periods, so if you've noticed other changes, they probably will start soon. I expect you already use a special toilet at school. Most toilets for people with disabilities are actually better equipped than normal

ones and you will probably find that there's a sanitary bin which you'll be able to use when you do get your period. It might be a good idea to check this out now.

Sometimes it can be hard for mums to start this type of conversation. You could try to raise the subject yourself by mentioning that one of your friends has just started her periods. But if that doesn't work you should tell your mum that you are worried. Your helper at school may also be able to give you some information – and show you how to use the sanitary bins, etc. SPOD (see the Further Contacts section at the end of the book) can help with information and advice for people with disabilities. Being in a wheelchair doesn't mean you will necessarily have any more problems than anyone else but it's obviously a good idea to get things sorted out so that you're ready to cope when the time comes.

I've had a discharge for ages but suddenly it has become heavier and really itchy. I've been washing about six times a day to try to get rid of it but it's driving me mad. I'm too embarrassed to tell anyone. What is wrong with me?
Although it's normal to have a discharge (which can be quite heavy at times) it should never be itchy, smelly or yellowy-green coloured. If it is, then you should get advice from a doctor or your school nurse. This may seem embarrassing but there are many common infections which can affect the vagina – it's just like getting a sore throat or throat infection.

Some girls and women suffer from "thrush" which causes a creamy, very itchy discharge. It is due to the overgrowth of a natural yeast bug. Sometimes this is set off by antibiotics you've taken for something else. Some people get thrush quite often, but there's nothing to be ashamed of. Do tell your mum or the school nurse. They will understand because most women suffer from this at some time. There are very good creams and pills available for thrush, most of which can be bought over the counter at a pharmacy. If you ask your mum, she'll probably get you something herself. In the meantime try washing with warm water and only use plain, unscented soap. Smelly soaps, scented bubble baths and wearing tight jeans can all make the irritation and itching worse.

I keep having these rows with my mum – often for no reason. I start shouting and saying things that I regret immediately, then I end up shutting myself in my room in tears. I hate it but I can't seem to say sorry and I don't know how to get out of it.

It sounds like your hormones! You're growing up and your body and emotions are changing. Many girls find they become very emotional or short-tempered during puberty.

You can try to stop the rows getting too out of control by either forcing yourself to walk away as soon as tempers get raised or by trying to count silently to 20 before you answer back. But if you and your mum do both hit the roof, try talking to her about this some time when you aren't feeling too uptight. I'm sure she'll understand what's going on and try to be more sympathetic.

CHAPTER 4

What Does Having a Period Really Feel Like?

In this chapter you'll find out more about:
* **Normal Symptoms of Periods**
* **Facts and Figures -**
  How Often Will I Have a Period?
  How Long Will They Last?
  Where Does the Blood Come From?
  How Much Will I Bleed?
  Why Does the Bleeding Stop?
  Isn't it Bad for You to Lose Blood Every Month?
  Will I Always Have Periods Now?
* **Myths About Periods**

Although it's normal to be nervous or a bit worried about how you'll cope, most girls are surprised at just how easy their first period is. There isn't usually much discomfort or pain and you probably won't even lose very much blood. In fact, you may not even realise you've had your first period! If you're already getting a heavy discharge then you may not notice any change at all – or you may just be aware of a few dark or rusty brown marks on your pants.

Your first period may only last for a few hours and, because they're often very irregular to begin with, you may not have another one for several months. So it's not surprising that some girls aren't sure whether they've really started or not!

You might be aware of a vague achy feeling in your lower back or a heavy dragging sensation in your tummy. Some girls find that their breasts ache a bit, and may even swell, for a day or so before their period starts. When your period begins, there'll be a feeling of wetness between your legs.

Less pleasant symptoms of periods are cramp-type feelings in your tummy or back. These are caused by the muscles around your uterus tightening and squeezing out all the broken-up old lining. Some girls have a headache or feel sick (nausea). You may also get a bit tired and irritable or bad-tempered. Often simple things like an early night, a warm bath, hugging a hot water bottle or taking a simple painkiller are enough to make you feel a lot better. For more information about coping with period pains, see Chapter Eight, The Next Few Years – Coping With Common Period Problems.

I didn't even realise I'd had my first period. I saw some brown stains on my pants but I thought I hadn't wiped my bottom properly. Then my mum was doing the washing and she asked me if I'd started. It went on like that for a couple of days then nothing else happened for about three months. Even then my periods were still very light and I didn't see anything that looked like proper red blood until about my fourth or fifth one.

Angie, 15

All my relations were over for some reason and I had a kind of funny stomach ache all day. It wasn't really a pain but something was definitely going on. Then I went to the loo and saw brown spots. I wasn't sure what it was so I checked it again later. By then it was red and obviously blood. I went to my room, got my sanitary towels that my mum had given me ready for when my periods started, and spent the rest of the afternoon brimming with pride. I waited until everyone went home in the evening then ran to my mum and told her! She gave me a massive hug and told me that I was now a "young woman".

Debbie, 13

It wasn't really a surprise when I started my periods, but I wasn't very pleased either. I was really into gymnastics and wearing a pad made life difficult. But at least it was over fast and I thought I coped really well. Then I started bleeding again two weeks later. I was sure something was wrong because I thought periods only came every 28 days. But I was too scared to tell anyone. It was only when my mum caught me trying to borrow some of her pads that she explained how periods can often be really irregular at first. Just as well she did because the next one didn't come for eight weeks!

Bella, 16

On our way back from a family holiday we stayed overnight in a bed & breakfast over a country pub. I was 11 at the time and, thanks to my mum, I knew all about periods. But it didn't stop me sobbing my heart out when I started. I went to tell my mum who also started sobbing and saying "my little girl is a woman now". My poor seven-year-old brother started to cry too as he didn't want to be left out! I'd already decided that I wanted to use tampons so my mother left me with a pack in the only loo in the B&B. I must have been in there for hours. I went through the whole box trying to get one to fit properly, and no one could go to the loo all evening.

Kristin, 15

Mine started when I was just 12 years old. I'd eaten a lot that day and thought I had indigestion or something. When I got undressed for bed that night I couldn't believe what I saw. I was so embarrassed. I went downstairs and waited around until everyone had gone to bed. I couldn't even say the words to my mum and had to show her my knickers. She was delighted and gave me a big hug and told me I was now a woman.

Gina, 16

I knew what was happening when I got my first period because we'd been taught about them at school, though my mum had never said anything about them. But, although I knew what a period was, I was still a bit shocked and grossed out when it happened.

Penny, 15

Normal Symptoms of Periods

Usual symptoms just before or during a period include:
- Low back ache.
- Tummy pains:
  - usually low down;
  - sometimes cramps (clenching pains that come and go).
- Tender or sore breasts.
- Feeling bloated or full up.
- Feeling a bit sick.

Everyone's different and not many girls have all of these symptoms. Also, each of these symptoms could mean something else, for example, you may feel a bit sick because you're going down with flu.

Facts and Figures

How Often Will I Have a Period?

Periods come roughly once a month, but it can take two or three years for them to settle into a regular pattern. For example, you might have your first one, then another one two weeks later, and then nothing for six months.

It's useful to keep a record of when you have your periods so that you can eventually work out your cycle and calculate when your next one is due. The cycle is the length of time between the **first day** of each period. Put a mark in your diary against the day your period starts and call it *Day One*.

Although the average length of a cycle is 28 days it could be anything from 21 to 35 days (3 to 5 weeks). You might be very regular or it could vary by a few days every month.

How Long Will They Last?

Periods can last anything from two to seven days but the average is about five days. You may find they're the same

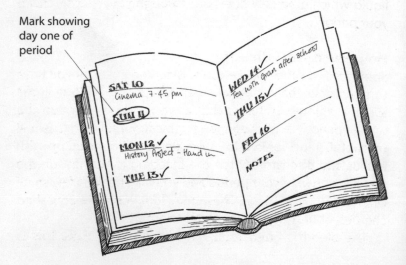

Mark showing day one of period

length every month or you could have a couple of short ones followed by a longer one.

When you mark your diary you could also put a tick for each day that you bleed so that you can see how long your periods are lasting. If you ever have a problem and need to talk to a doctor about your periods, it can be very useful to know this.

Where Does the Blood Come From?

Once you start your periods your uterus gets itself ready every month just in case it has to support a baby. During the second part of your cycle, the lining of your uterus thickens with extra cells and blood. This happens in case a fertilised egg comes along. If one doesn't appear, this lining starts to break up into a mixture of blood and dead cells. The muscles around the womb help squeeze it, pushing all the bits of old lining out. That is why you sometimes get a cramping feeling in your lower tummy or back. The blood and old cells from the lining mix with some mucus from your cervix, making an oozy liquid which gradually flows out through your vagina. This is your period.

How Much Will I Bleed?

Sometimes it can look like you're bleeding a lot, but you have to remember that what you see isn't just blood. In fact, the average amount of blood that a woman loses through the whole period is between one tablespoonful and a small teacupful. It just looks a lot more because it's mixed up with mucus and discharge. Often the bleeding is heaviest on the first day or two of your period and you may notice a few small clots or lumps of blood. These may look a bit like squashed cherries – but they are completely normal.

The blood is often redder in the first few days. This is

because it is fresher and flowing faster. As blood comes into contact with the air it turns a rusty brown colour, so the blood you see on a pad may look darker.

Why Does the Bleeding Stop?

For the last couple of days of a period the bleeding slows right down. This is because the womb has finished shedding its lining so all that comes out is that last little bit of blood, some dead cells and mucus. Then it's time for the lining of your womb to start getting ready all over again just in case it has to support a baby. Towards the middle of your cycle it starts getting plumper and thicker again. In turn this lining will also break away and come out, giving you your next period.

Isn't it Bad for You to Lose Blood Every Month?

Although it can seem a lot, you normally only lose a small amount of blood. Your body can usually replace it before your next period arrives but, because red blood cells are so important to your health, you need to ensure that you eat a good varied diet that contains plenty of iron. This is found in green vegetables, red meat and many breakfast cereals.

Will I Always Have Periods Now?

You'll carry on having periods all the time you're *fertile* (able to have a baby). They will go on until you are in your late forties or early fifties. Then they become less frequent until they stop altogether. This is called the *menopause*.

Myths About Periods

Over the years, many stories, "old wives' tales" or myths have grown up about periods, most of them completely untrue. You may have heard some of them yourself.

MYTH ONE – Everyone will know you're having a period.
NOT TRUE. You may feel a bit different inside but you certainly won't look it. As long as you keep yourself clean and change your pad or tampon regularly there's no reason anyone should know unless you tell them.

MYTH TWO – You can't have a bath during a period.
NOT TRUE. It's important to keep clean during your periods so if you like baths, go ahead. You might bleed a little but that doesn't matter and you're unlikely even to notice. Sometimes a nice warm bath can help back and tummy aches. Showering is absolutely fine too.

MYTH THREE – You shouldn't wash your hair during a period.
NOT TRUE. Washing your hair doesn't do you any harm at all. Some girls feel particularly run-down before or during a period and their hair can get greasy, so washing it can make them feel a lot better.

MYTH FOUR – You can't play sport during your period.
NOT TRUE. Even though you may feel a bit more tired than usual, exercise is great for making you feel good and easing period pains.

MYTH FIVE – You can't wear white clothes or tight jeans during your period.

NOT TRUE. Making sure you change your tampon or pad regularly will stop any embarrassing leaks on to light-coloured clothes. A tampon or one of the thinner pads is unlikely to show through tight jeans. See Chapter Six, What Should I Use? for more information.

Problem Page

I love swimming. Is it safe to go during a period?
There's no medical reason why you shouldn't go swimming when you have your period. The coldish water may slow down your period for a short time. But even if you did lose some blood, no one would notice a few drops in a swimming pool – it would be diluted by thousands of gallons of water! However, when you get out there could be a pinkish dribble running down your legs so you may want to get wrapped up in a towel very quickly.

Girls often decide they want to try tampons so that they can go swimming during a period. They can be worn in a swimming pool and no one will know.

I've just started my periods. Does this mean I have to carry stuff around with me all the time now?
It can take two or three years for periods to settle into a regular pattern so it's a good idea to have some emergency supplies available just in case. Keeping a couple of pads (the individually wrapped ones are great for this) in your bag or locker is a good idea. But, as you get used to your periods, you'll start to recognise the warning signs that mean one is on its way, so you can prepare for it rather than carry supplies all the time.

What happens if you go to the loo wearing a tampon? Doesn't it get in the way?
Not at all. Remember, you have three openings between your legs. A tampon goes in your vagina, but you pass urine (pee) from your urethra and stools (poo) from your anus or back passage. See Chapter Six, What Should I Use? for a diagram explaining exactly how a tampon fits inside you. Of course, going to the loo is a good opportunity to change your tampon – wash your hands before as well as afterwards.

Does the blood just gush out when you have your period?
No, it's usually quite gradual. Apart from blood, your period is made up of the broken-up lining of your womb plus some mucus. Altogether you only lose between a tablespoonful and a small teacupful of blood through your whole period – although it can seem a lot more than this at the time. Your period can feel heavy first thing in the morning or when you stand up after sitting down for a long time, perhaps after a lesson, but this is just the result of blood and liquid collecting and pooling while you are lying or sitting in the same position. When you stand up it comes out more easily for a short time. Playing sport or exercising also makes it come out slightly faster. Using the right thickness of pad or tampon will usually cope with this easily but, if you do feel you are leaking, try to get to a loo and check.

CHAPTER 5

Who Do I Tell?

This chapter covers:
- **Why It's Important to Tell Someone**
- **Telling Your Mum, Your Dad, Your Friends**
- **Telling Other Grown-ups and Asking for Help**

Why It's Important to Tell Someone

You may feel that periods are a very private matter and you don't want to talk about them to anyone. There's nothing wrong with that, but there are some very good reasons why you should let at least one person know that you've started your periods:

- However confident you are about coping on your own, there may be a time when you have a worry about your periods. It's important to know that there's someone who will understand and who will be able to offer help if you need it.
- Buying towels, pads or tampons costs money – and it could gobble up all your spare cash. If your mum knows that you've started, she'll probably help you out by adding them to her normal shopping list.
- If you feel really embarrassed, not telling anyone may seem like the easiest option – but it doesn't usually work in the long run. By avoiding talking about periods (or any other scary or personal matter) you can start to believe

more and more strongly that you couldn't ever talk about them. If there comes a time when you do need to get help from your mum or even a doctor, this makes life extremely difficult.

I told my mum when I started (I had to really as there was blood on my pants) but I didn't want to say anything to my friends. It was ages before I discovered that my best friend was having her periods and then it was only because she was desperate to borrow some pads when she started unexpectedly. Once we realised that we were both having them it was a big relief knowing there was someone else who understood.

Kaye, 13

I kind of knew that my period had started because I had a stain in my pants, but then it came on much heavier during the night and I had blood on my nightclothes and on the sheets. I was really embarrassed but my mum was great. She said it was no big deal and explained that soaking things in cold water was the best way to loosen the blood stains before they go in the wash.

Chloe, 14

There was this big thing at school about who'd started and who hadn't. It was awful because, as more and more people started, anyone who hadn't felt very left out. Even the boys knew who had and who hadn't and I hated it. Part of me wanted to start so I'd be like everyone else and the other bit of me dreaded it because everyone would know.

Sam, 15

I've got two older sisters and although my mum told me the general stuff about periods I got all the really useful info from my sisters. They'd always talked about what was going on and what it felt like so I suppose I was lucky growing up knowing that periods were completely normal. They suggested which towels I should try and then encouraged me to have a go with tampons.

Lois, 14

Telling Your Mum, Your Dad, Your Friends

Telling your mum

Maybe your mum has told you lots about periods and growing up. Or perhaps she just left a leaflet for you to read or maybe mentioned in an embarrassed way that she assumed you were doing "growing up and stuff" at school. Just like girls, mums cope with the whole business of bodies and puberty in different ways. Some are really up-front, others feel embarrassed and some feel anxious that they won't be able to explain it properly. But one thing is certain. Your mum will be waiting for you to start your periods and will want to help you.

The surprising thing is that so many girls find it so hard to tell their mums.

My mum didn't tell me much about periods but she did check that we'd covered it at school, then said that I shouldn't be afraid to let her know when I started. Well I have – but I am. I've had two periods now and I don't know how to tell her.

Claire, 11

My mum's always talked to me about periods but when I had my first one I didn't know what to say to her. I kept thinking I'd wait and say something the next time, but now they've been going on for months and if I say something she'll want to know why I didn't tell her before.

Sophie, 12

If you've started, or think you're about to start your periods but are worried about telling your mum, try one of these:

- Bring the subject up indirectly by asking your mum how old she was when she started her periods or mentioning that a girl at school has just started.
- Go shopping with her, pick up a pack of pads and ask if you can put them in the basket.
- Leave a note on your bed saying "Dear Mum, could you please get me some sanitary pads when you go shopping?"
- Leave a copy of this book lying around!
- When you see an ad for pads or tampons on TV or in a magazine, ask her if she thinks they're any good.
- Offer to help with the washing up, then, when you're standing side by side, take a deep breath and say "Mum, I've started my periods."

If you have already had several periods, but have still not told your mum, you may find it particularly hard to raise the subject. In this case a little white lie along the lines of "I think I may have already had a period but I just wasn't sure" can work wonders. But remember, the more directly you approach the subject, the less likely it is that your mum will miss the point or fail to catch on. You want her to know you've started – that way you don't have to pluck up the courage to say it all over again!

Me and my best friend started the same day which we still find amazing. We were 13 and it was the big netball tournament. I was at her house and started getting stomach ache but tried to ignore it because I was so anxious about the game. When I went to the toilet there was blood. I realised what was happening but just wished it would go away. I didn't tell anyone for two months and then I left a note on my mum's bed. She came into my room that night and talked to me about it all. I felt much better about things then. It was a couple of months later that I told my friend and she asked when it had started, and she said how freaky it was because that was the same day that hers had come. I felt more "normal" then!

Helena, 16

I started when I was 11 – the day before my first day of high school. I was really embarrassed about telling my mum. She gave me towels and a few days later produced a book she'd got from the library on the subject. Each month a new packet of towels would appear in my drawer just before I came on, and basically my mum never mentioned it again. I've never found it very easy to approach her about personal things but usually one packet wasn't enough, so I'd end up buying more out of my pocket money and paper-round earnings. It took me ages to pluck up courage to go into my local chemist and buy my own. It seemed that someone I knew would always come in just as I was getting them off the shelf!

Caz, 17

Cracking the Code

Mums get embarrassed too – and sometimes you may not realise what your mum is trying to ask you or talk about. For example:

"You do know you can talk to me about anything?"

"Is there anything you want to tell me?"

"Are you sure you're feeling OK?"

"You know, you're really growing up."

can ALL be attempts to bring up the subject of periods!

Telling your dad and the rest of the family

Some girls feel really close to their dads and are happy to tell them what's going on. But this may be the last thing you want. Sometimes though, mums get carried away and yours may feel that everyone should know you've "turned into a woman". She will probably want to mention it to your dad because it's the sort of thing that parents like to know and (believe it or not) feel proud about. Even if they're not told, nosey brothers and sisters may easily find out by seeing pads in the bathroom or in the shopping.

But just because they know doesn't mean to say you have to talk about it if you don't want to. It's your business and you have a right to privacy. If you feel that things are getting out of hand, have a word with your mum and explain that, while you don't mind people knowing eventually, you'd prefer it if she didn't broadcast the news to the whole street!

What if you don't have a mum?

Some girls live just with their dads. You might think this could make dealing with periods tricky but, strangely enough, most men are so anxious about getting this right they go to a lot of effort to make sure their daughters have information and a supply beforehand. They may ask a female friend or relative to help with this or perhaps they'll resort to the "Here's a book you might like to read" approach. Perhaps they'll even use this one!

Even if he hasn't managed to bring up the subject, your dad will be anxious that you should get as much help and support as possible. So don't be scared to say that you've started or you think you are about to begin your periods. Sometimes you do have to be the one to bring it up. If your dad really looks as if he can't cope with all this girl stuff, either ask him to suggest a female friend that you could talk to or reassure him that you've already got things in hand by talking to the school nurse or a friend's mum.

Telling friends

You may want to share this news with your very best friend but, before you do, think carefully about how many people you really want to know. Is she likely to go spreading it all round the school? Would you mind that? If the answer to these questions is yes, maybe you should think twice before telling her.

Often it's very useful to be able to talk about periods and feelings with a group of close friends. It means there's always somebody you can borrow pads from in emergencies, and you can also swap experiences. Take care, though. Some girls delight in telling horror stories about periods and it's easy to get the wrong idea from listening to someone who's deliberately trying to impress or scare you. Remember that everyone's different – just because one girl has a bad time with her periods doesn't mean to say that you will too.

My friend told me as soon as she started her periods. She was really excited and I was pleased for her but I also felt left out.

Before that we'd been the only two in our group who didn't have them, but it didn't matter because we had each other. All of a sudden she seemed to be joining in with everyone else and leaving me behind. It made things really awkward between us for a while.

Kath, 14

I started my periods really young, just before I was ten. Although my mum had realised that I was growing and told me what to expect, I still felt peculiar because none of my friends were even thinking about periods. I wanted to be able to talk to them but I was scared they would think I was weird or something. It wasn't until we had a lesson at school that my best friend asked me if I'd started and I was able to say something about it. After that it was much easier.

Sally, 11

Telling Other Grown-ups and Asking for Help

School nurses and teachers

Obviously you don't have to tell any grown-ups at school that you've started but it can be useful knowing that there's someone there who can help. School nurses (if your school has one) are usually absolutely brilliant at this. They've always got supplies they can give you and they know all the problems and worries that can go with periods. They can give you lots of reassurance and advice.

I was 11 when I started my periods. It was a Tuesday night, my aunt was round and we were having egg and chips for dinner (don't ask me what that has to do with it – it just sticks in my mind). I knew what it was, but was still embarrassed about telling my mum. Anyway she told my aunt and my sister and, before I knew it, it was like I'd won a competition or something. But it was the next day at school that freaked me out. I was quite proud that I was a "woman" now and told all my close friends. I thought periods were easy-peasy, but then I was sitting in class and felt myself "flooding" so I rushed to the loo and realised I'd forgotten to bring anything with me (it must have been all the excitement). I went to the medical room and the head teacher's secretary gave me this huge towel – bigger than anything my mum had ever mentioned. It felt really weird but it did the trick. But I NEVER EVER forgot to take pads with me again!

Sophie, 15

If you start your periods when you're particularly young, perhaps when you're nine or ten and still at primary school, then your school may not have disposal bins in the girls' toilets. It may even be difficult to lock a cubicle door in order to change a pad. In this case, it can be extremely helpful if a teacher knows. Probably the best thing is for your mum to have a word with them but, if not, don't be scared to say something yourself. They can often arrange for you to use the staff lavatory whenever you need to. The big advantage of them knowing is that you can then put your hand up and ask to be excused without having to explain – possibly in front of the whole class – what the problem is.

Asking for help

Nobody is expecting you to go around wearing a big shiny badge saying, "Hey, I've started my periods," but there may be times when you need a bit of help in a hurry. Many women will be happy to help you out. For example, if you were at a friend's house and you started suddenly, you could always ask her mum for help. Or if you were out shopping you could go to the nearest ladies' toilet in a shop or coffee bar. They may have a machine that sells packs of single pads but, even if they don't, you could ask any other woman in the loo if they could help you. Most women carry an emergency supply of pads or tampons in their bag and will be only too happy to let you have one.

Problem Page

My mum talked to me a lot about periods and always said I should tell her as soon as I started. So I did. Big mistake! She immediately told my dad and my brothers and sister. They all kept grinning at me! And, as if that wasn't bad enough, she keeps on telling them every time I come on as if I'm some sort of performing puppy! How can I get her to stop doing it?

Show her this letter – immediately! You know she's only trying to make you open and totally unembarrassed about periods – but it's not working. It's one thing your family knowing that you're well on the way to becoming a woman but there's no reason for them to have monthly updates! Get your mum on her own and tell her how great it is that she's so understanding and can offer you so much help – but could she please make it a bit less public?

The boys at school are really silly about periods. They think they're a big joke and they're always looking in girls' bags to see if they've got any pads in them. If we say anything that they don't like, they laugh and say that we're moody because we're "on". We all hate it! What can we do?

Boys can be a real pain sometimes! They obviously don't understand about periods so they try to make them into a joke – and that ends up hurting you. It sounds as though they need a bit of basic education, and to learn some respect. Get a group of girls together and talk to a sympathetic teacher. Explain what is happening and suggest that the boys have a lesson or two about puberty and the changes that take place in both sexes.

I'm really worried about starting my period while I'm in school. We have some male teachers and I'd hate to have to explain to them if I had to go to the loo or something. Any hints?
Men often do get embarrassed about periods but sometimes this can work to your advantage. You shouldn't have to explain everything, just put your hand up and ask to be excused. It's unlikely that a male teacher will want to know the details!

My little brother is always going through my things and he found a box of tampons in my drawer. I don't think he knew what they were but he realised they were something private. He pulled them out and started swinging them around, showing them to his friends. Now they all laugh at me and I'm so embarrassed. Can you help?
They're making fun of you and that is cruel, but they're more interested in seeing you blush than what's actually in that box in your drawer. Talk to your mum about this and get some support. Then do your best to ignore your brother and his annoying mates.

I've started my periods but there's no privacy in our house for me to change my pads. I share my bedroom, and my younger brothers and sisters are always barging into the bathroom when I'm in there. I've tried talking to Mum but she says I'll just have to get used to it. Is she right?

Please talk to your mum again. Coping with your first periods can be worrying. The last thing you need is the fear of an audience bursting through the bathroom door. Ask your mum if you can get a simple lock fitted. She may argue against it because she's worried about the smaller children getting themselves locked in the loo but you could either place a bolt high up on the door where they couldn't reach it or get the type of lock that can be opened from the outside by a grown-up in an emergency. Maybe you could offer to put some money towards it to show you are serious.

I'm so embarrassed. My mum and dad split up three months ago and Dad moved to a flat. I'm going to stay with him in two weeks and I just know my period will arrive while I'm there. I'll die of embarrassment if he finds out. What should I do?

Don't panic! Your dad does know all about periods. But the easiest thing for you to do is be prepared. Pack some pads and, when you get to your dad's place, ask if you can have a special drawer to keep your things in, so you don't have to bring all your stuff each time you visit. Then you can keep your spare pads, undies and a toothbrush ready for when you need them.

When it comes to getting rid of any pads, make sure they are well wrapped up in plastic bags (or one of those special scented bags you can buy in the chemist) and pop them in the rubbish bin (see Chapter Six, What Should I Use? for more about the disposal of sanitary products). Do try to let your dad know if your period is making you feel a bit miserable or you are in pain. He will probably be really pleased that you can talk to him about this sort of thing.

CHAPTER 6
What Should I Use?

This chapter covers:
- **Sanitary Products and How They Work**
- **Pads, Towels and STs**
- **Tampons**
- **How Often Pads and Tampons Need to be Changed**
- **Getting Rid of Pads and Tampons**
- **What to Use in an Emergency**

If you go and look at the shelves in a supermarket or chemist's shop you'll see lots of different types of sanitary product. These include pads/towels (sometimes called sanitary towels or STs) and tampons. Sometimes they're under a sign saying "feminine hygiene". If you can't see them, ask a shop assistant where the sanitary products are and they'll understand what you mean.

Most girls are bought their first pads or towels by their mum – or they get a free sample at school.

I want to be ready for when my periods start but I don't know what to buy. There are so many different sorts. It is really hard to choose.

Jane, 11

My mum bought me some pads but they're enormous! She said I should ask my friends what they use but I'm too embarrassed.

Annie, 12

I've been using pads that my mum buys me and they're OK but I'd like to try tampons when I play hockey. I'm a bit scared and think my mum might not approve.

Jess, 12

I used to send for free samples of tampons and sanitary towels from magazines. I kept them in a shoe box at the back of my wardrobe so I was prepared for the big day.

Sally, 16

Remember, women all over the world have periods, so sanitary products are big business and there's a lot of money to be made selling them. Companies spend fortunes on advertising and giving away free samples. Manufacturers rely on people sticking with the type they first use. This may not always be best for you, so shop around and don't be afraid to try something different.

Sanitary Products and How They Work

Sanitary products work by soaking up the blood lost during a period, so the most important thing they have to be is absorbent. Years ago, perhaps when your great-grandma was a girl, women used rags and sponges which they washed out before using them again. Modern sanitary products are obviously more convenient and hygienic than this!

The options
There are basically two types of things you can use –
pads/towels or **tampons**.

Pads, Towels and STs

Pads, towels and STs (short for sanitary towels) all mean the same thing and they all come in all sizes and thicknesses. They go inside your pants, between your legs to soak up blood from your period. Even the thinnest are often called towels on the pack label, though many girls call them pads. The sort of towels and STs that your mum probably used at your age were much thicker and bulkier than the ones you can get now. If you look along the supermarket shelf that stocks sanitary products, you'll see packs in all shapes and sizes. They range from long, thick wedges of fibre to very thin, flexible pads that are hardly thicker than the lining of your pants.

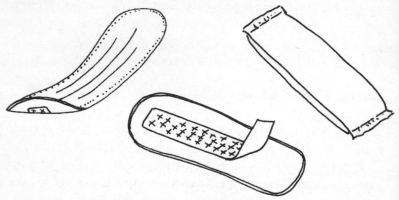

Pads usually have a sticky pad on one side so that they can be fixed to your pants. You need to peel off the shiny paper on the sticky bit before you can use them.

Different sizes

The more old-fashioned towels are filled with fibres like cotton wool. They are absorbent but also bulky to wear. The more modern, thinner pads often contain special fibre or gel which expands as they get wet and holds a large amount of liquid. They use the same type of technology as disposable babies' nappies.

Most brands of pads and towels come in a variety of different sizes, ranging from something like "ultra thin" to "super plus" or "night-time", which are the most absorbent of all. Some brands also offer a special longer type of pad which some girls find very effective.

Leaking

All sanitary products leak if they are not changed in time, but most girls find some more reliable than others. That's one of the reasons why it's a good idea to try out different brands to see what suits you best, and which type you find most comfortable and reliable. Some pads have a waterproof backing that helps stop the blood seeping through on to your underwear. This can be useful. The downside is it can also make you feel sticky or sweaty because it stops air getting to your skin.

"Wings" and fragrance

Some pads have "wings". These are sticky-backed tabs on either side of the pad that you can wrap around the middle bit of your pants to hold it in place more securely. Some girls find these very successful but others complain that they feel uncomfortable or that the extra sticky bits tug at their pubic hairs!

Some pads have added fragrance, which may make you feel more secure. However if you're washing a couple of times a day anyway, you shouldn't have any problems with unpleasant smells. And wearing artificial fragrances close to your skin all day can sometimes make you feel itchy.

Tampons

How tampons work
Tampons are about the size and shape of a finger. They have a thin string attached to one end and they go inside your vagina with the string hanging down between your legs so that you can pull the tampon out when you need to change it.

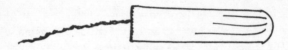

As the tampon gets wet it expands, soaking up the blood. The big advantage of tampons is that they are worn inside your body, so you don't feel anything inside your pants and, providing you change them often enough, they're less likely to leak. Many girls feel more secure playing sport or wearing tight clothes when they're using tampons. You can also swim whilst wearing one as long as you're able to change it very soon after coming out of the water.

How to insert a tampon
Putting in your first tampon can seem a bit scary but it does give you a good opportunity to understand how your body works. The tampon needs to go inside you with the bottom

end (with the string) about two or three inches past the opening of the vagina. It can help to put a finger into your vagina first to feel which direction it points – usually upwards and backwards towards the back of your waistband.

Tampons feel uncomfortable if they haven't been pushed in far enough. There is a tight ring of muscle around the entrance to the vagina, which you can feel with your fingers. If you don't push the tampon past this, then the muscle clenches on the tampon – that's what causes the discomfort.

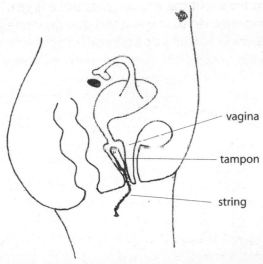

vagina

tampon

string

Most tampon packs include very good instructions and diagrams. These are very useful for new users so it's worth reading them.

It's often easier to put a tampon in when you're either crouched over the loo or standing with one leg up on the lavatory seat. Have a look with a mirror if you're not sure where the opening is. Don't be embarrassed – get to know your own body!

Different sizes of tampon

Tampons come in different sizes starting from mini (extra small) right through to super plus (extra large). Don't worry – you don't need to know how big your vagina is because that isn't why they're different sizes. The idea is that the larger tampons will expand more and cope with a heavier flow of blood.

When you use tampons for the first time it's best to try the smallest size. They'll be easier to insert. Then, once you're used to them, you can try out the larger sizes as you need them. For example you may want to use a larger tampon overnight or when you're playing sport to make sure there are no leaks.

Rounded ends and applicators

Not all tampons look the same. Some have flat ends and some are gently rounded. Others come with applicators. Those without applicators need to be pushed in with your finger – the rounded ones are often easier to insert.

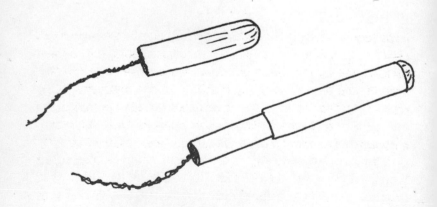

Applicator tampons come in two cardboard tubes that fit tightly inside each other. You insert the thicker tube (containing the tampon) into the entrance of your vagina. Then, as you push the tubes together the tampon is pushed out and up into your vagina. If you don't like touching yourself this can be a big advantage – but some girls find applicators uncomfortable to use and there's the added problem of having to dispose of the cardboard tubes as well the used tampons. Although they do flush down the loo they're not very eco-friendly.

I used towels for years because I just couldn't get the hang of tampons. Then one holiday we were all going to go swimming so I decided I just had to try one. It took me half an hour of puffing and shoving and discarding dozens of the things, but I managed to get one in eventually and I ran about shrieking the house down. My dad was shouting at me for making so much noise but my mum was so proud. Since then I've never looked back and I don't know how I managed without them.

Lena, 16

I was very skinny and under-developed so I didn't start my periods until I was 16. When I was 14 I thought I was missing out so I sent off for a free sample of tampons and tried to insert one. I walked around all afternoon with my friends in agony because I hadn't pushed it up far enough and it was sticking out. I pretended to my friend that I was having period pains because I was too embarrassed to admit that I hadn't started yet. Sad or what!

Cagsy, 18

Pads Versus Tampons – Good and Bad Points

Good Points

Pads	*Tampons*
Easier to use for beginners	You can swim, bath and shower with them in
Special night-time ones are brilliant	The extra big ones work very well
Pads with "wings" can be very secure	You can wear tight clothes
	They're smaller and easier to carry about
	Can be flushed down the lavatory if necessary
	Less messy and less risk of any smell using them

Bad Points

Pads	*Tampons*
They aren't easy to dispose of	Fiddly to use for beginners
You can't swim with them	Slight risk of toxic shock syndrome (see page 77)
Thick ones can be bulky and show through tight clothes	Can be easy to forget to remove the last one at the end of your period
There's a risk they can be smelly if not changed regularly	Once you start to leak it can be very noticeable
Large ones are bulky to carry around or keep in your bag or locker	

How Often Pads and Tampons Need to be Changed

Whether you use pads or tampons, you'll probably need to change them at least four times a day. This helps you feel fresh and secure and stops any unpleasant smells. When your period is heavier – often the first couple of days – you'll either need to change them more often or use a thicker pad or larger tampon. For the last day or so of your period you may bleed very little and only need a thin pad. Many girls and women use two or three different types of sanitary products during the average period. They may start with extra thick pads or tampons for a day or two, then go on to thinner ones, finishing with the thinnest type of panty-pad. Some brands of pads and tampons now come in useful packs containing a variety of different sizes.

If using tampons it is very important that you change them regularly. See the warning box on *toxic shock syndrome* at the end of this chapter.

At night

As you don't want to have to get up to change during the night, or leak on to the bed, you usually need to wear something thicker and heavier. This can feel a bit strange, particularly if you aren't used to wearing pyjama bottoms or pants in bed. But you'll soon get used to it.

Some towels are specially designed to last you all night long. They're usually a lot bigger than you'd want to wear during the day but they do the job! You could use tampons at night if it feels more comfortable with them – but don't forget to change them first thing in the morning. The other alternative is to use a tampon and a pad together.

Getting Rid of Pads and Tampons

Tampons and some pads (it's important to check on the packet) can be flushed down the loo. If they don't disappear the first time, wait for the WC to refill and flush again. However, although these products are designed to be flushed away, many people feel that this isn't very eco-friendly. Non-dissolved or broken down sanitary products play a big part in the pollution of our oceans. Closer to home they can also sometimes clog up the plumbing or drains!

Pads and towels that can't be flushed away (and that means most of them) need to be wrapped up tightly and either disposed of in the dustbin or in one of the special bins or incinerators in ladies' lavatories. Many public ladies' lavatories have little bags available for you to wrap them in. But it's a good idea to carry a couple of bags yourself. Old plastic carrier bags are fine for this or you can buy packets of special scented plastic bags. This may be a good idea if you've got to carry them around for a while but make sure you like the smell of the bags first! However, freshly used sanitary products don't smell very much and there should be no problem about disposing of them in a bin as long as they're wrapped up well.

What to Use in an Emergency

So what do you do if your period starts unexpectedly? Firstly, don't panic! It happens to everyone at some time, and you'll usually be able to manage. If there are any other girls or women around don't be scared to ask if they have an emergency supply in their bag. After this, you'll probably start to carry an emergency supply too! But if there's no one around to help, you can make a pad from folded loo paper or tissues. And if the worst happens and there's none available you can be inventive. Anything that will soak up the blood for a short while until you get home or to a shop will do the trick. How about a sock? No one will know if you don't tell them!

Problem Page

If I use tampons does it mean that I won't be a virgin any longer?
In medical terms, no. A virgin is someone who has never had sexual intercourse. Putting a finger or a tampon inside you doesn't mean to say that you aren't a virgin, though some cultures have rules and beliefs that say girls shouldn't put anything into their vagina before marriage.

I'm 14 and I'd really like to use tampons but my mum won't let me. She says you have to be much older. Is this true?
You can use tampons at any age. Tampons can be very useful, particularly if you want to go swimming or play sport. Perhaps your mum doesn't use them herself or is worried that you would find them difficult to manage. Some people are very frightened of tampons because of the risk of toxic shock syndrome (see page 77). This is very, very rare and you can make it even less likely by taking simple precautions like changing your tampons regularly and always making sure you remove the last one at the end of your period.

Try talking to your mum again and ask her what it is that particularly worries her about tampons. Perhaps she would compromise and let you use them for sport and swimming.

Can I have a bath or shower during my period? If so, should I wear a sanitary pad?

Getting into the water wearing a pad would be soggy and uncomfortable – and not much use! But keeping clean during your period is important and will make you feel better as well. Luckily blood doesn't flow out very fast during a period and the effect of getting into water often seems to slow it down even further. So while you may notice a pinkish tinge between your legs in the bath, a bath or shower at least once a day is still a very good idea. Apart from that, washing thoroughly between your legs with warm water and possibly a very mild soap is a good idea.

Make sure you have a clean pad ready for when you get out of the bath and maybe some tissue or loo paper to dry between your legs to stop you getting any blood on the towel.

Of course, if you use tampons you can wear them in the bath or swimming or whatever – but you still need to change when you come out.

What if I leak and the blood goes through on to my clothes?

This doesn't happen as much as you might expect. But, if it does, you can usually rely on other girls or women to help you out. Often they'll be aware of it before you and will usually try to tell you quietly so you can get to the nearest loo. You can always tie a jumper round your waist or, if the worst comes to the worst, your friend can always walk closely behind you so no one else will see. But, even if they do, it's nothing to be ashamed of. Boys may be cruel and make fun but that's only because they don't understand the realities of being a woman!

What if I'm at a friend's house and need to change my pad but there's nowhere obvious to put it?
Take it off, roll it up tight and wrap it in some loo paper. If you've got a plastic bag with you (always a good idea) tie it up tight in that as well. Then, after you've washed your hands, either take it outside and drop it in the dustbin or put it in the main kitchen rubbish bin. If your friend's mum is around say "Is it OK to put my pad in there?" She's bound to understand what you mean and be able to help you out.

I haven't started my periods yet but when I do, I'd really like to use tampons. Would it be dangerous to try them out now?
It wouldn't be dangerous but it might be a bit uncomfortable. Most girls start off using pads although some quickly move on to tampons. If you want to try one out now choose the very smallest size and put a blob of spit on the end, as this will help it to go into your vagina more easily. Make sure you push it up high enough (see the instructions for putting in the tampon) and then try walking round for about half an hour to get used to the feeling. It should be comfortable. If not, you know you probably haven't put it in far enough.

Don't leave the tampon in any longer than half an hour because when you haven't got a period there's no liquid for it to soak up and this makes pulling it out uncomfortable. If you can't seem to get it in properly try checking the direction of your vagina with your finger (it goes upwards and backwards). You could also use a little petroleum jelly, e.g. Vaseline, to help it go in more smoothly, but this is waterproof so it wouldn't be any good when you need to use a tampon for real.

I'd really like to use tampons but I'm scared the string might break and I wouldn't be able to get them out. Does that ever happen?

Not very often – although it isn't impossible. But don't worry, it's usually fairly easy to get the tampon out. Either crouch over the loo or stand with one foot on the lavatory seat. Then feel inside yourself with your fingers. It may feel a bit weird at first but breathe deeply and try to relax. Try again, pushing your fingers in as far as you can and you'll feel the tampon. Then you can pinch it and bring it out. If this doesn't work, the Practice Nurse at your doctor's surgery will be able to help you. Ring her straight away.

What would happen if I forgot to take a tampon out at the end of my period?

Leaving a tampon in after your period has finished can increase the risk of infection or even toxic shock syndrome (TSS). However, it's an easy mistake to make and many women have done it at some time. You might start to notice a nasty-smelling discharge after a few days, which would continue until the tampon was removed. You should try to remove the tampon yourself, but if it is stuck, or if you have developed a temperature or any pain in your tummy or lower back, or a rash, then you should see a doctor immediately. **This could be a medical emergency.**

But remember, millions of women use tampons all their lives without any problems.

Toxic Shock Syndrome (TSS)

This is an extremely rare but serious illness. You can get it when you wear tampons, but about half of all cases are NOT connected to using tampons – sometimes boys get it too.

Although most people do recover from toxic shock syndrome, it has caused some deaths – so it's really important you look for help straight away if you think you (or someone you know) might have toxic shock syndrome. **EARLY TREATMENT SAVES LIVES.**

TSS may seem a bit like flu with some or all of these symptoms:
- High temperature.
- Vomiting.
- Diarrhoea.
- Sore throat.
- Dizziness.
- Fainting.
- A blotchy red rash (like deep sunburn).

If you think you have toxic shock syndrome the first thing you need to do is remove your tampon, but then you must see a doctor immediately – even if it means going to the Accident and Emergency Department of a hospital. Tell them you've been having a period and using tampons.

You will be less at risk from TSS if:
- You never use tampons at all.
- If you do use tampons, only use them for the very heaviest days of your period.
- Change your tampons regularly – if you use one overnight, change it first thing in the morning.
- Always remember to remove the last tampon as soon as your period is over.

This is Polly's story:

Polly was aged 15 when she had toxic shock syndrome. The day before she came into hospital she had been out roller-blading. When she came home she had a headache and aching muscles, and instead of going out to her cousin's party in the evening as she had planned, she had a quiet night in watching "Friends". She went to bed early but awoke the following morning feeling dreadful, with vomiting and diarrhoea. She went back to bed but her mum became worried over the next few hours when she developed a red rash which looked like sunburn. Her mum decided that Polly needed to see a doctor urgently so she took her to the Accident and Emergency unit at the local hospital and, after being examined, she was admitted to a hospital ward. At first the doctors weren't sure what was wrong with her, but after hearing that she was in the middle of a period and using tampons, they thought it might be toxic shock syndrome. They started treating her at once and, although she was very unwell for several days, she was very lucky and went on to make a full recovery.

CHAPTER 7
Am I Different Now?

This chapter covers:
- Parents Expecting You to be "Different"
- Looking After Your Health: Eating, Sleeping and Keeping Clean
- Spots and Acne
- Hairy Problems
- Fertility

Parents Expecting You to be "Different"

Lots of girls worry that getting their period means they're going to turn into someone different overnight. Well-meaning parents often say things like, "You're a grown-up now," or even start treating you differently – and expecting you to act differently. But you aren't a different person! Growing up is a long process and getting your first period is only one small part of it. It just happens to be a bit more noticeable than some of the other changes that have been taking place in your body over the last couple of years. So, although your body is behaving a bit differently, inside you are still one hundred per cent you.

When I told my mum that my periods had started I thought she'd be pleased, like me. I suppose she was a bit, but then she kept going on about how now I'd have to start acting as a grown-up and be really "careful" – whatever that means! I couldn't understand why, just because I'd started having periods, I was suddenly supposed to keep my room really tidy and act differently at home!

Leah, 14

I was quite nervous telling my mum but she was great. But then she told my dad. He made this big thing about coming up and congratulating me because I'd "turned into a woman". I didn't know where to look or what to say. Probably he was just as embarrassed as me but I still wish he hadn't made a big thing of it.

Ashley, 13

I started my periods when I was ten. I couldn't believe it as it was only three weeks earlier that I'd been teasing my older sister for starting hers. Maybe I should have left her alone! I was too embarrassed to tell my mum and I used folded up toilet roll in my knickers until the bleeding stopped. I eventually told her when I had my second period. She was a bit shocked but said that she'd also started her period when she was 10, so she sat down and gave me the talk about why we have them and stuff. I already knew this from school really, but I listened anyway. It was strange because I still felt like a little girl and I was afraid that I'd be treated differently.

Kay, 15

Reasons why parents might act like this

Seeing their children grow up can make mums and dads feel quite strange. Because it happens so gradually, they may not notice it very much and they can persuade themselves that you're still "their little girl". But when periods start, it's an obvious change and they have to come to terms with the fact that you're turning into a young adult. This can make them feel old themselves as well as worried for your safety and your future. Just at the time when you feel you're growing up and expecting more freedom, they can suddenly start to become over-protective.

Looking After Your Health: Eating, Sleeping and Keeping Clean

Many girls find that, once their periods start, they want to know more about looking after themselves and staying healthy.

Eating and diets

As your body is still growing, it is very important you eat a healthy diet (and enough of it) so you can develop strong muscles and bones. You need more food than an adult because growing uses up calories.

Just as your breasts start to develop, your hips, tummy and bottom can also become more rounded. It's a normal part of turning into a woman, but many girls panic and think they need to lose weight to get back to the thinner shape they used to be. This is not a good idea. Crash diets never work because you nearly always put all the weight back on again immediately afterwards. They can also be dangerous. If you are overweight or fatter than you want to be, the best solution is to change your diet slightly. Eat more healthily – try to be sensible about what you eat. Cut down on chocolate, crisps and snacks and fill up on pasta, baked potatoes, fruit and veg. At the same time try to do more exercise. Even if you don't like sport at school you might still enjoy swimming, dancing, cycling or even walking the neighbour's dog.

If you're still worried about your weight or shape then talk to your school nurse or your doctor. They'll be able to advise you on a healthy diet and give you an idea of what sort of shape you should be aiming for. Remember that very few people really look like supermodels. Part of your size and shape is inherited from your parents – and there's only so much you can do to change it!

Sleeping and rest

You also need to get enough sleep. You may notice you get tired around the time of your periods so it's a good idea to make sure you get some early nights. Many teenagers have no trouble sleeping – they just have difficulty doing it at the right time! If your mum is always nagging you about late nights and never being able to get up in the morning, she may have a point. The occasional late night is fine but it's much better for you to keep to a regular pattern of sleep. That way you'll find it easier to fall asleep when you do go to bed, rather than tossing and turning until the early hours of the morning.

Lack of sleep interferes with concentration and performance so you'll find it much harder to focus at school and, if you're always tired, your schoolwork and marks will suffer. Some people also find that lack of sleep makes them more likely to catch any colds or bugs that are going around.

Sweaty smells and keeping clean

Everyone sweats when they get hot but it doesn't make you dirty or smell bad. However as the sweat dries and then gets stale, it can smell very unpleasant indeed. When you go through puberty and your body begins to change, your hormones make your sweat start to smell different. Having an all-over wash or, even better, a bath or shower every day keeps your skin clean and fresh.

It may be tempting to use strong-smelling soaps or shower creams but this isn't usually necessary. Warm water and mild soap work just as well.

Many girls find their hair becomes greasier during puberty, particularly around their periods. Washing it regularly helps. Sometimes using lots of styling products, like mousses and gels, can make the problem worse. Swapping between a gentle shampoo and a deep-cleansing shampoo can help keep your hair looking good and free from the build-up of styling gunk.

It's around this time that most people start using anti-perspirants and deodorants. These come as sticks, roll-ons and sprays and are usually used on your armpits. Deodorants help stop the sweat smelling by either disguising the smell or by slowing down the going-stale-and-smelly process. Anti-perspirants work by tightening up or clogging the pores on your armpits so that you don't sweat so much in the first place. There are many different types and combinations available. If you get a reaction to the chemicals or scent used in the deodorants and antiperspirants, your skin can go red and itchy. That's a sign to stop using this type at once, wash it off and wait at least 24 hours before trying anything else.

"Intimate hygiene" products

You may see these for sale or advertised. They're often deodorants or scented powders or body sprays for use between your legs. If you are washing regularly then you shouldn't need these. And because the skin in this area is so delicate, strong scents and chemicals can cause unpleasant irritations and reactions.

Spots and Acne

Your skin starts to produce more oil during puberty, and it is very common to get spots. When these happen all the time it's called acne. Keeping your skin clean and using a toning wash or lotion will help dry off the extra oil and close up the pores. This helps heal up the spots and prevent more forming. However, if you still have a problem, there are many excellent creams and medicines available.

If you've already tried lotions and creams from the super-market, try asking the pharmacist in any large chemist for their advice. They keep stronger creams and ointments behind the counter which they can sell you. If they don't work, talk to your school nurse or doctor. Doctors can prescribe creams or pills that will help most sorts of acne. You may have to take them for several weeks before you see an effect – and carry on taking them until you've grown out of the spot problem – but they do work!

Hairy Problems

At around the time your periods start, you'll also notice that you're growing more hairs on your body. This is perfectly normal but, particularly if they are thick and dark, some girls prefer to get rid of them – at least in the places they show. Whether you do or not is up to you; there's nothing wrong with body hair and many women resent the idea that they "should" shave their legs or their armpits. However, if you do decide to have a go at taming your hairy bits, you need to know how to do it.

There are lots of creams available that work by dissolving the hair but these are very strong and, if you don't follow the instructions carefully, you can leave chemical burns on your skin. Very painful! Waxing is very effective, but is expensive to have done professionally and fiddly to do yourself. Shaving is easy and convenient to do on underarm hair but more tricky on your legs. One drawback is that once you've started, you usually have to continue – at least until the winter comes and you go back to wearing tights and trousers.

Don't be tempted to shave your arms as this will be uncomfortable and it won't look nice. If you have hairs on your breasts these can usually be plucked out carefully with tweezers, but if there are more than a few you should ask for professional advice from your school nurse or doctor.

If your pubic hair gets so bushy that it shows round the edges of your swimsuit, you can trim it – very carefully – with small scissors. Don't be tempted to shave or wax your pubic hair. Apart from being difficult to do, it's also very itchy and uncomfortable when the hair starts to grow back.

Fertility

Starting your periods means that your body is starting to produce eggs (see Chapter Two for more info.). An egg will be released every month about 12 to 16 days before your period. This means you are *fertile*. If you had sex with a boy and sperm met up with your egg, you could get pregnant and have a baby. That's one reason why parents may suddenly seem very over-protective or worried about you!

Just because you're producing eggs doesn't mean to say you're ready to have or look after a baby. It is illegal for a boy to have sex with a girl before she is 16 (under 17 in Northern Ireland), and most girls under this age are not ready to take on the responsibility of looking after another human being.

Problem Page

My tummy sticks out a lot and it makes it difficult to wear nice tops. Should I go on a diet?

Strict diets are dangerous at your age because your body needs a wide range of foods to allow your bones and muscles to carry on growing properly. However, cutting back on junk food and snacks like biscuits and chocolate won't do you any harm as long as you fill up with three proper meals a day. Don't forget breakfast – it's really important!

Choose some exercises to help strengthen your tummy muscles. Sit-ups and tummy crunches are good and can be done in the privacy of your own room. Swimming and dancing are also effective.

My legs are very hairy and I want to shave them. I'm not quite sure what to use but was thinking about borrowing my dad's electric razor.

Not a good idea! Although it might work well at first, it would quickly get clogged up with the hair from your legs (which are a lot bigger than his chin hairs) and he wouldn't be very pleased.

If you want to shave your legs, the easiest way is to use a simple disposable plastic razor. Lather up your legs with soap and water or shaving foam first, then pull the razor gently but steadily upwards in long, slow strokes. Rinse it off between each stroke, jump in the shower or bath afterwards and you'll have lovely smooth legs. But remember – once you start shaving, the cut ends of the hair can feel very stubbly so you may need to carry on doing it regularly.

I started my periods three months ago and I've just started going out with my first boyfriend. Does having my periods mean that I'm now ready to have sex?

Absolutely not! The law says that the age of consent for girls is 16 in England, Wales and Scotland, and 17 in Northern Ireland. It is unlikely that you would be ready to cope emotionally with it before then anyway. Having sex puts you at risk of sexually transmitted infections as well as pregnancy. These are all things you need to be able to talk about with your boyfriend before things get that serious between you. If the idea of this makes you feel uncomfortable, it shows you really aren't ready to go this far yet.

About six months before my periods started I began to get very hairy. Now I've got thick, black hair all over my legs and arms, up my tummy and I'm also getting hairs on my chest and face. I hate it and people keep laughing at me at school. What can I do?

The same hormones that start your periods off also change your body hair, making it thicker and darker. This can be a bit of a shock at first but most people get used to it. If you look at your mum or the other women in your family you'll get an idea of what's likely to be normal for you. Your mum may have had the same worries so try talking to her about it.

However, in some girls hairiness can be much worse. A rare cause is polycystic ovary syndrome. Other symptoms are irregular periods and increase in weight. Unfortunately some girls with these symptoms are too embarrassed to seek help. This is a shame because there is very good medical help available for this problem so, if you are worried, do ask your mum to go to the doctor with you.

I've got really bad spots all over my face, neck and back. I've tried lots of creams which haven't helped. My mum says it's because I eat too much junk food. Is she right?
Eating lots of greasy or sugary junk food doesn't do your health any good – but it doesn't actually cause spots and acne. What does cause them is the extra oil produced by your skin due to the change in your hormones during puberty. Everyone has bacteria on their skin but when the pores on your face start to get blocked up with oil, the bacteria can infect the swellings, causing nasty red and yellow spots.

It's important to keep your skin clean, and using a special anti-bacterial wash from the chemist can help. But if it's still a problem it's worth asking your GP for advice. Talk to your mum and see if she can go with you. Doctors can prescribe effective creams and pills for spots, but it may take a few weeks for them to work.

I have real trouble getting to sleep at night. In the mornings I can never seem to wake up and my mum goes on at me. What's wrong?

Difficulty getting to sleep (sometimes called insomnia) is common at your age. You can help it by trying to stick to a regular routine. Getting up early may feel awful but you will certainly be sleepy that night! Try having a warm bath, some camomile or herbal tea, or a milky drink or bowl of cereal before going to bed. Don't watch TV or play computer games last thing at night as they can over-stimulate you and keep you awake. When you're in bed, close your eyes and try to imagine that you can see thick, black velvet. Concentrate on breathing slowly in and out and feel yourself being drawn towards the imaginary velvet. This helps you relax and empty your mind of other thoughts so you can drift off to sleep.

CHAPTER 8

The Next Few Years – Coping With Common Period Problems

This chapter covers:
- **Period Pains and Pre-menstrual Syndrome (PMS)**
- **Heavy Bleeding**
- **Irregular Periods**

Most of this book is about getting ready for your periods and coping with all the normal questions you'll have when they first start. Many girls quickly settle into a regular pattern and everything goes smoothly, but there are some common problems that you might encounter in the first few years – or indeed, at any time while you are having periods. These are covered in this chapter.

Period Pains and Pre-menstrual Syndrome (PMS)

Most girls feel a bit uncomfortable either just before or during the first couple of days of their period. They have what people call "period pains" but usually they aren't too bad. The important thing to remember is that if the pains get too uncomfortable or difficult, there are lots of ways of helping to make yourself feel better.

Some girls feel particularly tired at this time or get miserable and cross or feel extra clumsy. When this happens before your period begins, it's called pre-menstrual syndrome or PMS. You've probably heard people talking (or even making unkind jokes) about it.

I can always tell when I'm about to come on because apart from feeling teary whenever there's something sad on the news, I start bumping into things – or knocking my wrists or elbows on doorframes.

Karen, 17

How to cope with normal PMS and period pains

Most of these feelings are easy to cope with by trying one or more of the suggestions below. But see the box on period pains (page 93) for information on painkillers and getting medical help.

- Make sure you get lots of extra sleep for a couple of days before your period starts and during it. It's a time when your body needs a bit of extra loving care, so looking after yourself makes a real difference.

- If you feel a bit low or miserable, talk your feelings through with your mum, school nurse or a close friend.

- Don't skip meals at this time; if your tummy is empty, your blood sugar level can quickly drop, leaving you feeling shaky and miserable. Some girls find it easier to eat smaller meals but have extra snacks (e.g. yoghurt, cereal, fruit) in between.

- A warm bath or a hot water bottle can help cramping or aches. Hot drinks, e.g. herbal tea, can be good too.

- Although you may not feel like it, exercise and stretching can release some of the cramps and make you feel much better. This doesn't have to mean going for a ten-mile run or playing hockey! Dancing (even on your own in your bedroom) is a brilliant form of exercise, but so is a brisk walk or some quiet yoga. There's an extra bonus too – when you exercise, your brain releases chemicals into your blood that give you a natural boost.

See the box on period pains for what to do if these suggestions don't work.

I used to find it really hard to cope with my stomach cramps and backache on the first couple of days of my period but I've learnt that lying in a nice, warm bath and burning some aromatherapy candles to relax me makes a big difference.

Susie, 14

I used to have real trouble with PMS. I'd get very depressed and moody but I changed my diet and make a point of eating much more fruit during the day. It's really made a difference and I hardly notice PMS now. And the pain is better too. I am aware though that I eat much more on the first few days of my period. I just get so hungry.

Katie, 17

Treatment for Period Pains

If self-help remedies (see above) don't work, try:

Over-the-counter medicines that you buy from your chemist or supermarket, e.g.

- Paracetamol – 1–2 tablets may be taken every 4–6 hours (definitely no more than 8 tablets in a 24-hour period).
- Ibuprofen (Brufen or Nurofen) 1–2 tablets 3–4 times a day. Ibuprofen works by reducing prostaglandins – the hormones that cause the painful cramps in the uterus during a period. Ibuprofen can make asthma worse so, if you have asthma, it's important to check with your doctor before using it.

WARNING: Girls under 12 should never take aspirin for period pains as it can occasionally cause severe problems. Many people also find it less effective than paracetamol or ibuprofen.

If over-the-counter medicines are not helpful you should talk to your GP (more about this in Chapter Nine, Getting Help). GPs are able to prescribe:

- Stronger painkillers which you cannot buy over the counter.
- Other drugs, such as Ponstan, which are particularly effective for period pains. They work best if you start taking them before your period is due.
- Tablets containing hormones to help bring your cycle under control.

WARNING: It's very important to tell your doctor about ALL tablets and medicines you are taking – even if you bought them yourself. Always look at the small print on the label as some things you can buy may contain several different ingredients, e.g. a mixture of paracetamol, caffeine and codeine. If you are also taking something else containing paracetamol you could "overdose" without realising it.

Heavy Bleeding

Doctors say that someone has heavy periods if they:
- soak more than six of the largest sized pads or tampons per day for more than one or two days, OR
- if the bleeding goes on for more than seven days with each period.

Most girls find this happens sometimes, but if you get it regularly, e.g. three times in a row or for more than a quarter of your periods, then you may start to get side effects from losing too much blood. You need the red blood cells in your blood to carry oxygen around your body. If you lose too much blood it can lead to a condition called anaemia. This isn't very common (particularly if you eat a good mixed diet) but, if you did have anaemia, it could cause you to feel:
- faint;
- tired;
- headachey.

If you think your periods are too heavy or if you're getting any of these symptoms, it's a good idea to ask your doctor for advice. This isn't as embarrassing as it sounds. Your doctor will ask you some questions about how long you've been having periods and how long each one lasts. They may take a small sample of blood from your arm to check for anaemia. For more information on talking to doctors, see the next chapter.

If your periods are heavy for more than three months in a row it's very important to tell your doctor. They will want to ask you questions and may want to check your blood. Depending on the results they may give you iron tablets (which work by boosting the red blood cells and making you feel less tired and faint) or possibly by giving you a short course of hormone treatment which will help control and lighten your periods. For a few severe (and very rare) cases further treatment from a hospital specialist may be necessary.

I never had much of a problem with period pains until I got to the age of 16. I kept telling my mum and teachers about them but they wouldn't believe me, telling me not to make such a fuss. We had a school nurse but she only came in one day a week in the morning and you had to book an appointment so she was always booked up. For some reason I felt scared to go to the doctor because I thought I'd be wasting his time.

One day at school my period started in the morning and by 11 a.m. I was in real pain and my head was pounding. I had to do something so I left the classroom and went to the school secretary's office (normally to be avoided, but I was desperate!). She took me to the nurse, interrupting her appointment. The nurse sat me down and gave me a sugary drink and rang my doctor to make an appointment, and also rang my mum. When Mum arrived, the nurse told her that I wasn't well at all and that she was to take me to the doctor's that afternoon. My mum looked so guilty! We went to the doctor's and apparently what I was going through was quite common and easily sorted by taking Ponstan tablets. So every month when I got my period and felt the slightest twinge, I took one of the pills. From then on I had no trouble at all. If only I (or my mum) had known how easily the pain could be stopped, I would have gone to the doctor straight away.

Jenny, 18

Irregular Periods

Some things can affect your periods and make them more irregular. Worry or stress, e.g. about exams, can either bring them on or delay them. Lots of girls find their period comes early if they go somewhere hotter than usual (not very convenient on holidays!) and travelling to high altitudes can also affect them, making them heavier or more frequent.

Periods can also sometimes be delayed by normal illnesses like colds and flu or simply by going on a strict diet. It could be your body's way of telling you that you aren't eating enough!

When periods stop

Once your periods have settled into a more or less regular pattern they won't stop unless there's a good reason. And it's important to find out what that reason is because it could be affecting your health.

I've been having regular periods for more than two years but all of a sudden they've stopped. I'm really worried and my tummy feels a bit swollen and uncomfortable.

Claire, 14

If your periods suddenly stop and you miss more than one, it's important to talk to your doctor or your school nurse. The most common reason for periods to stop is that you are pregnant. So be prepared for some questions about this and, if there's any risk at all that you might be pregnant, it's very important to get help as soon as your first period is late. Your school nurse or doctor can help you with this and you can ask them to keep it confidential. You can also get more advice from special young people's health clinics, e.g. Brook (see Further Contacts).

There are other reasons why periods stop. A strict diet or a sudden increase in exercise can make your periods stop. This is usually a warning sign that you're overdoing things.

When a period is late or delayed, it's normal to feel a bit bloated and achey in your tummy and lower back, but if you're getting severe or unusual pains (i.e. unusual for you) then always ask for medical help.

Problem Page

I had period pains so I bought some tablets from the chemist that were especially for this. They helped the pain but they made me feel a bit peculiar, so I don't know whether I should take them or not. What do you suggest?

Have a look at the labelling on the pack of tablets you bought. They'll probably contain a normal painkiller like paracetamol or ibuprofen but they may also have a large amount of caffeine in them as well as other ingredients. Caffeine, the same chemical that you get in tea and coffee, is a stimulant and can help some painkillers work better – but it can also make you feel jittery or sick. Some of the other ingredients can have the same effect. You'd probably do better sticking to a simple painkiller. Paracetamol is good and so is ibuprofen, but if you've ever had asthma, you should check with your doctor before using it.

I find my periods really difficult – not because they're painful but because my tummy and breasts feel swollen and I can't fit into my normal clothes. Is there anything I can do?

This is a very common problem – girls and women all over the world suffer from it! Often it's caused by your body retaining more water than normal in the days leading up to and during your period. It can make you feel very bloated and it's particularly noticeable in your breasts and tummy. Some girls find that taking Evening Primrose Oil capsules for a week before their period helps, or you could try a gentle herbal diuretic (anti-water) pill. You can buy both from a pharmacy but, in either case, ask the pharmacist for his or her advice first. Your doctor may also be able to suggest or prescribe something – but lots of girls and women do end up having to cope by wearing a slightly larger bra or looser waistbands during those days of the month.

Why do I get so hungry just before and during my period? I usually try to eat a really healthy diet but for that week I just want to eat lots of chocolate and crisps and junk food. Is this normal?
Food cravings – particularly for sweet or fatty things – are a normal and irritating part of pre-menstrual syndrome (PMS). It's probably connected to your body's blood sugar level which seems to drop easily during these days. When it goes low you may start to feel a bit shaky or light-headed and your brain begins to tell you you're hungry. Unfortunately, eating foods with a high sugar or fat content may make you feel better for a little while but the effect doesn't last long. Your blood sugar will quickly drop back down again making you feel even worse than before.

The answer to this is to try eating small amounts of healthy food at regular intervals during the day. If you're worried about your weight, cut back a bit on your main meals (but make sure you still have a good breakfast) and have healthy snacks like cereal, yoghurt or fruit or even the odd biscuit every couple of hours. It should make you feel a lot better.

My periods are very heavy and, although I use tampons, the "super plus" type don't always work. Could I use two tampons at once to soak up more blood?

No – this isn't a good idea! Tampons are designed to work on their own so they can swell up freely in all directions. If you push two together they won't work nearly as well. There's also the risk that one might get pushed up too far into your vagina so that it's difficult to get out or may even be forgotten about. This may lead to a nasty discharge and possibly an infection.

Either change your tampons more frequently or use a larger size of tampon with a small pad as back-up. Remember, if heavy bleeding goes on for more than two days each period, you should ask your doctor for advice.

I started my periods last year and I never know when I'm going to get the next one. My mum says it's because I don't eat properly. I'm a vegetarian but sometimes that's difficult because I'm the only one in our house who is. Is this likely to be affecting my periods?

It often takes two or three years for your periods to settle down into a regular pattern but it's also very important that you eat a good, balanced diet so that your body can keep on growing healthily. There's nothing wrong with being a veggie but cutting out meat from your diet means you have to make sure you get protein and minerals like iron and calcium from other foods. Just eating the veggie bits of family meals probably won't be enough for you. Get hold of a book on vegetarian diets or see Further Contacts for more information. Have a look at it with your mum and try to plan meals that either the whole family can eat or special extras to make sure you're getting the right sort of foods.

If you're losing weight on your diet, that could be why your periods are playing up. Otherwise, eat healthily and don't worry unless they haven't settled down in another year or so.

CHAPTER 9
Getting Help

This chapter covers:
- **People You Can Ask for Help**
- **Signs That Mean You Need to See a Doctor**
- **What Happens When You Visit a Doctor About Your Periods**

Although periods are a normal part of growing up, they can still take some getting used to. Most girls find they need a bit of help and advice at some time. Perhaps you'll just need to talk to your mum to make sure that the stains in your pants really do mean your periods have started. Or you may want some advice on the best way to get rid of used pads. Often you may already know the answers to these questions (particularly if you've read this book!) but talking it through with someone else and knowing that they agree can make you feel a lot more confident. However there may come a time when you have a more serious worry that your mum or your best friend can't help you with. This is the point when you have to think about talking to a doctor and getting medical advice.

This chapter talks about people you can easily ask for help, gives some suggestions about those you may not have thought of asking, and explains how to talk to and get the best advice possible from your doctor.

People You Can Ask for Help

If you have a worry or a question about your periods there's usually someone obvious around who you can ask, such as:

- Mum/stepmum/foster mum/carer;
- Big sister/auntie/grandma;
- Best friend.

I'd been having periods for about six months and I wanted to try using tampons but was embarrassed to say anything to Mum. I knew my sister used them because I'd seen them in her bag so I asked her and she was great. She showed me the leaflet that comes in the pack and explained to me about keeping relaxed and practising putting them in. Also, when Mum found out I was using tampons too, she didn't mind at all because she knew I'd had good advice.

Lisa, 13

There are problems at home so I'm in care at the moment. I'd just moved to a new foster family when my periods started. I was really scared – I knew what it was but I didn't want to have to say anything, yet I had to because it was such a mess. My foster mum was great and showed me a special shelf in the cupboard where she kept spare pads and stuff and even clean underwear for an emergency. She said that it's common to start at embarrassing times and that worry can bring your period on. Knowing that someone understood and didn't make a big deal about it made all the difference.

Sally, 12

I kept getting leaks on my clothes with my period and I thought it was just me, but my friend told me about some pads she wore that were stretchy and seemed to fit better. She gave me one to try and after that I started buying them myself. They were much better.

Sam, 13

WARNING: Friends can give lots of good advice but sometimes, even if they mean to be helpful, things can go a bit wrong.

All my friends talked a lot about their periods and I felt a bit left out until I started too. They kept going on about how much they were bleeding and how tired it made them. So I wasn't surprised when my periods were quite heavy and lasted for more than a week at a time. Whenever I mentioned it, my mates all said that they had the same problem, but eventually I started to feel really ill and Mum took me to the doctor. It turned out that my periods were far too heavy and I'd become anaemic. That's why I felt so tired all the time. I don't think my friends meant to mislead me – but I do think they were probably exaggerating things a bit. I wish I'd realised that earlier!

Hattie, 13

People you may not have considered asking for help:

- Dad;
- Friend's mum/family friend;
- Youth club or Guide leader;
- School nurse;
- Teacher;
- Pharmacist.

Asking your dad about something like periods may seem a strange idea, but fathers are often very concerned about this part of their daughters' lives and, even if they do sound a bit embarrassed when you raise the subject, they'll do their best to find out the answers for you.

Talking to a friend's mum can sometimes be easier than talking to your own mother. It may be a bit less personal or embarrassing. Most parents understand this – you may even find your friend asking your own mum for advice herself!

If you do want to bring up the subject but you aren't sure how she'll take it, try saying something direct like "Can I ask you a question about periods?" or "Can I ask you something private?" This lets her know that you want to discuss something serious with her – and gives her a chance either to tell you that's fine or to make an excuse if she doesn't feel comfortable with it.

When I started my periods my mum bought me some pads and then kept getting me new ones every month. But after my first period I didn't come on again for ages. I was too embarrassed to tell her though. Then I went on a sleepover at my friend's house. My mum insisted I took some pads with me "just in case". My friend's mum saw them and quietly gave me some plastic bags, saying that if I wanted to get rid of any used pads I could just wrap them up and give them to her. She was so normal and calm about it that I found myself telling her that it had been nearly three months since my last period. She explained that it was really common to have big gaps when you first started. I just wish somebody had told me that earlier!

Trudy, 14

A youth leader or Guide leader will usually be able to give you some help and may get you more information such as leaflets if you need them. Sometimes it's easier to ask a person like this because they don't belong to school or home. Usually anything you ask will be kept private between you and them, but if you're not sure about this, you can ask them if you can have a private talk or if you can speak to them "in confidence". This means they are agreeing that they won't tell anyone what you tell them – or at least not without your permission.

A school nurse or teacher can also be very helpful. If you don't think your own teacher is very sympathetic, you could try speaking to the games teacher or another one you like and trust. School nurses are very clued up about periods and often have emergency supplies and useful leaflets and books for you too. Again, if you're worried about other people finding out, start off by asking if you can speak to them in private or "in confidence".

I used to get really bad period pains and feel quite sick for the first day or two. Sometimes I had to ask to leave the classroom and I got the feeling that some of the teachers thought I was making it all up and just trying to bunk off. Eventually the school nurse had a word with me and basically asked what was going on. I found her really easy to talk to. She encouraged me to keep a note of the dates of my periods and mark which days were particularly bad. Then she said I was to take it to the doctor and ask for some more help. In the meantime she had a word with the teachers and after that they were much nicer to me. If I felt bad I could just go to the medical room for a while and everyone understood.

Sasha, 14

A **pharmacist** is the person (often in a white coat) who is in charge of giving out the medicines in a chemist's shop. They may not seem like the obvious person to ask but they've had training in how drugs work and, if you're having problems with period pains, they can be really helpful. Of course it's a bit nerve-wracking asking something like that in front of lots of other people. What you can do is wait your turn in the queue then ask if you can speak to the pharmacist in private. Most pharmacies have a quiet area where you can talk and get advice without other customers overhearing. They can often answer any immediate worries and suggest the best type of pain relief if you need it.

Signs That Mean You Need to See a Doctor

Although most problems and worries can usually be easily solved, there are times when it's important to talk to a doctor. This may seem scary or embarrassing but GPs (family doctors) are very used to dealing with all the worries and confusions that go with growing up. They'll be happy to help put your mind at rest. And they'd usually much rather you asked them for advice – even about something very simple – than worry about it on your own.

You should see a doctor if you have:
- Period pains or sickness that are bad enough to stop you going to school, taking part in sport or going out at the weekend.
- Vomiting with periods.
- Periods that last more than seven days each month.
- Very heavy bleeding, i.e. regularly soaking through more than six of the largest size pads or tampons in 24 hours – especially if this goes on for more than two days every period.

- Periods happening more than once every three weeks.
- Bleeding between periods.
- Periods that stop after they have already settled into a regular pattern (remember this can take up to two or three years).

Also, if you feel that all your friends have started before you – and particularly if you haven't got any of the other signs of puberty, e.g. breast buds, or hair under your arms or between your legs, then it's often a good idea to have a check-up just to put your mind at rest.

WARNING: If you are using tampons and you have symptoms of toxic shock syndrome (TSS) during your period, you must see a doctor AT ONCE.

Signs to look out for include:
- High temperature.
- Vomiting.
- Diarrhoea.
- Sore throat.
- Dizziness.
- Fainting.
- A red blotchy rash (like sunburn).

Tell a grown-up, take out your tampon and either go straight to your doctor or a hospital Accident and Emergency unit.

For more information see the section on TSS at the end of Chapter Six.

If you decide you want to see your doctor, it's usually best to tell your mum or your carer first. They'll want to support you and possibly go with you to the surgery. However you don't necessarily have to go with someone else. Some GP practices have rules about how old you have to be before you can see a doctor on your own but, if you're not sure about this, you could ring the surgery receptionist and ask. Many doctors are very aware that young people will want to talk about things in private and often try to make it easy for them. For example, when you visit for something like a sore throat or ear infection they may suggest your mum waits outside for a few minutes. This gives you a chance to talk about anything that's been worrying you.

One doctor told us:

At our practice we try to make sure that anyone over the age of about 12 has the chance to talk to a doctor or nurse on their own if they want to. When they come in for something routine like a throat infection we often suggest that they pop back a week later on their own just so we can check they're getting better. This gives us a chance to ask if there's anything else worrying them and helps the young person get used to talking to us without feeling everything has to be said through their mum or dad.

If you do go and see a doctor about your periods try and take a list of your dates and how long the periods have lasted for. Take your diary or copy them off your calendar.

Some girls are worried that a doctor will want to look at them between the legs or examine inside their vagina (called an internal examination). Internal examinations are very unlikely to be necessary for young girls with period problems, but if a doctor did suggest it, they would also explain why they needed to do it and you would have the right to say no. If you have a male doctor they should ask a female nurse or receptionist to stay with you in the room whilst you are examined.

What Happens When You Visit a Doctor About Your Periods

First, they'll ask you quite a few questions. It's a good idea to think about these beforehand so you're ready with the answers. These include:

- How long is your cycle? This means how many days is it between **the first day of each period**?
- How long (how many days) do your periods last?
- Do you bleed particularly heavily on some days of each period – if so, on how many?
- How many pads or tampons do you soak through on each of the "heavy" days?
- Do you ever pass any blood clots – bright red blobs of thick blood a bit like squashed cherries?
- Do you have pain and if so where is it (e.g. back, tummy)?
- How long does the pain last for and what do you do to help stop it?
- Do you ever feel sick or faint with your periods?
- Does this stop you doing normal activities?

When you've answered these questions the doctor may want to:
- Look under your lower eyelids to check for signs of anaemia.
- Feel your tummy – particularly if you're getting pains there.
- Measure your height and weigh you.

Depending on the problem, the doctor may:
- Say that everything is normal.
- Suggest you try some medicine, e.g. stronger painkillers.
- Suggest you try some hormone pills to try to make your periods less heavy and more regular.

If you're nervous about talking to your doctor, remember:
- Doctors are very used to dealing with period problems so there's no need to feel embarrassed.
- If the doctor starts to use big medical words you don't understand, just ask what they mean and they'll explain.
- It can really help to have someone with you. If you don't want to go with your mum you can take a friend.
- Even if you're under 16, everything you tell the doctor should be kept confidential. This means that they won't repeat it to your parents or anyone else without your permission. If you're still worried about this then ask the doctor if your talk will be confidential or private. They should be able to reassure you.

I started my periods when I was 12. The first year they were quite light and I didn't have much pain or trouble. Then they began to become more painful, and one day at school my tummy-ache was so bad that I nearly fainted. The school nurse gave me some paracetamol tablets, but as they didn't help very much she suggested that I go and see my doctor. The thought of visiting the doctor frightened me – I didn't know what they would do, but my mum persuaded me that it was the best thing. The young female doctor was very sympathetic. She asked a few questions about when my periods started, how long they lasted, how often they came and how heavy they were. She asked what the pain felt like, where it was and how long it went on. Then she asked what medicines I had already tried and gave me a prescription for a different painkiller.

I was relieved that the visit was so straightforward and that the doctor didn't ask anything really embarrassing or want to examine me. I started taking the new pills and now, three months later, period pains are no longer a problem.

Emily, 14

I was 16 and the only girl in my class who hadn't started my periods. I was sure there was something the matter with my "insides" and started to panic that I'd never have a period and never be able to have a baby. I was really embarrassed but finally my mum realised how upset I was and persuaded me to go with her to talk to our GP. The doctor was really calm and matter-of-fact. She asked me if I'd noticed any of the changes of puberty, e.g. if my breasts had started to develop or if I had any hairs between my legs. I told her that I had got a few pubic hairs and also some under my arms. She asked if she could look at my breasts and that was fine because she told me they were developing normally and that my periods would probably arrive quite soon.

She was right. My first period came three months later.

Jenni, 18

Problem Page

My periods often come a long time apart and now I haven't had one for three months. My mum says I should go and see the doctor and I know she's probably right but I'm scared he'll ask embarrassing questions about me and my boyfriend. I know I'm not pregnant but I don't want to have to talk about things like that. Do you think I should go?

It's important to understand that when a girl's periods suddenly stop, a doctor has to wonder whether she's pregnant. You may feel the question is embarrassing or insulting but it is a sensible question for a doctor to ask. He or she will usually try to do it sensitively, e.g. if you go to the surgery with your mum, they may suggest that you'd like to talk on your own for a few minutes. They'll probably ask you if you think there's any chance you could be pregnant and all you have to say is no, you're sure you're not. There's no reason for them to ask you any personal questions about your boyfriend but, even if they do, you don't have to answer if you don't want to. Periods can stop for other reasons and it's important that you find out what has caused this as soon as possible.

I get really bad cramps with my period and my friends all say I should take some paracetamol or something, but I hate swallowing pills. Even the thought of it makes me want to gag. Is there anything else I can have?

Lots of people have problems with pills. Luckily you can get many medicines in liquid form or as soft, jelly capsules which aren't so difficult to swallow. Paracetamol can be bought as a syrup and is often used for small children. You can ask the pharmacist in the chemist's shop for his advice. Remember to read the label carefully and never take more than the recommended dose.

My periods have been getting more and more painful and nothing I take seems to help. I've told my mum but she says I'm just making a fuss and it's something I'll have to put up with. I'd really like to see a doctor but my mum won't take me. Can I make an appointment on my own?

Although some doctors' practices have recommended minimum ages, there's no set age that you have to be before you can go and see a doctor on your own. So yes, you can ring and make an appointment. The fact that you want to go and see your doctor shows that you are grown-up enough to be seen and treated, but they'll probably still encourage you to tell your mum what's happened. However, they won't go behind your back and say something to her unless you give them permission.

And finally

Although this book talks a lot about the problems you can have with periods, it's important to remember that most people cope very well without any major difficulties. We hope that you will have found the answers to most of your questions in our book but, if there is still something worrying you, there is always somewhere to get help. If you don't feel able to talk to your mum, doctor, or any of the other grown-ups we've suggested – or if they can't answer your question – do try one of the organisations, helplines or websites listed in the Further Contacts section.

Further Contacts

Note *– numbers beginning 080 or 050 are Freephone.*

For more information about puberty and periods contact:

Family Planning Association (FPA)
England and Wales   0845 310 1334
(helpline open 9a.m. to 6 p.m. weekdays)
* Scotland   –   0141 576 5088
* N. Ireland   –   028 90 325 488
www.fpa.org.uk
– for advice on all aspects of sexual and reproductive health,
  including periods and puberty, etc.

Brook
0800 018 5023
www.brook.org.uk
– a national counselling organisation fo young people,
  offering free, confidential (private) advice on periods,
  puberty and any other issues about sex.

ChildLine – *England, Wales, Scotland and Northern Ireland*
ChildLine, Freepost 1111 NATN, London E1 6BR
0800 1111
www.childline.org.uk
– 24-hour counselling and advice service for children and
  young people.

The Line (ChildLine's service for young people living away
  from home or in care)
0800 88 44 44 (weekdays 3.30–9.30 p.m., weekends 2–8 p.m.)

Childline – *Eire* (run by the ISPCC)
Ireland Freephone 1800 666 666
– 24-hour counselling and advice service for children and
young people.

Sexwise
0800 28 29 30
www.ruthinking.co.uk
– confidential helpline for teenagers on sex, relationships
and contraception.

Who Cares? Trust
LinkLine 0500 564 570 (Mon, Weds, Thurs 3.30 p.m. to 6 p.m.)
www.thewhocarestrust.org.uk
– support and advice for young people in care.

Acne Support Group
PO Box 9, Newquay, Cornwall TR9 6WG
0870 870 2263
www.stopspots.org
– offers advice and support for people suffering with acne.

Toxic Shock Syndrome Information Service (TSSIS)
24–28 Bloomsbury Way, London WC1A 2PX
020 7617 8040
www.tssis.com
– 24-hour recorded information line on symptoms and
treatment of toxic shock syndrome.

www.wiredforhealth.gov.uk
– lots of useful information for teachers about health and
growing up.

If you are depressed or are having emotional difficulties contact:

ChildLine – *England, Wales, Scotland and Northern Ireland*
0800 1111 (open 24 hours)

ChildlIne – *Eire*
Freephone 1800 666 666

Samaritans
08457 90 90 90 (open 24 hours)
email: jo@samaritans.org

Get Connected
0800 096 0096 (open 3 p.m. to 11 p.m. every day)

No Panic
01952 590545 (open 10 a.m. to 10 p.m. every day)
0808 808 0545 (for their freephone helpline)
– help for anxiety, phobias and panic attacks.

For information about nutrition and diet:

www.wiredforhealth.gov.uk
– website covering all aspects of health for young people.
 Lots of useful information under healthy eating.

The Vegetarian Society
0161 928 0793 (open 9 a.m. to 5 p.m. Monday to Friday)
www.vegsoc.org
– useful booklets and nutritional information for young
 people wishing to remove meat from their diet.

Viva!
0117 944 1000
www.viva.org.uk

Eating Disorders Association
0845 634 7650 (for 18-year-olds and under)
 (4 p.m. to 6.30 p.m. weekdays, 1p.m. to 4.30 p.m. Saturday)
0845 6341414 (adult helpline)
 (8.30 a.m. to 8.30 p.m. weekdays, 1 p.m. to 4.30 p.m. Saturday)
www.edauk.com
e-mail: helpmail@edauk.com (over 18 years old)
        talkback@edauk.com (under 18 years old)
– support and advice for anyone experiencing difficulties
 with eating.

Addresses parents might find useful:

FPA
0845 310 1334
  (helpline open 9a.m. to 6 p.m. weekdays)
www.fpa.org.uk
e-mail: fpadirect@fpa.org.uk
fpa, 2-12 Pentonville Road, London, N1 9FP
– to order publications and for a free copy of fpa's catalogue

Parentline Plus
Helpline 0808 800 2222
www.parentlineplus.org.uk
– help and information for anyone involved in caring for
  children.

Trust for the Study of Adolescence
01273 693311 (9 a.m. to 5 p.m. Monday to Friday)
www.tsa.uk.com
– national research organisation providing information and
  resources for professionals working with adolescents. Also
  resources available for parents.

YoungMinds – Parents' Information Service
Helpline 0800 018 2138
www.youngminds.org.uk
– national charity committed to improving the mental
  health of all children and young people.

Glossary

Absorbent   Able to soak up liquid.

Acne   Spots and red pimples on the skin. Often starts around puberty. Mainly affects the face, back and chest. Lots of treatments are available.

Age of consent   The age at which a young woman can legally agree to have sex; 16 in England, Scotland and Wales, 17 in Northern Ireland. Any boy or man having sex with her before this age is breaking the law.

Anus   Sometimes called the back passage. The opening in your bottom where stools (poo) come out.

Areola   The darker circle of skin around your nipples.

Bacteria   Organisms (bugs) which cause infection. Often treated with antibiotics.

Breast buds   The small, sometimes tender, lumps that develop under the nipples at the start of puberty.

Breasts	Boobs, tits, bosoms or busts. The breasts grow during puberty. They are made of milk-producing glands and fatty tissue. If you have a baby they produce milk.
Cervix	A tight ring of muscle round the opening from the uterus (womb) into the vagina. Literally means the neck of the uterus.
Clitoris	A small, very sensitive, pea-sized area in front of a woman's vagina, near where the labia minora meet.
Cycle	A regular sequence of events. For example, the menstrual cycle happens when an egg is released roughly every four weeks.
Diuretic	Something which causes you to pass more urine (i.e. wee more). You can buy diuretic tablets from a chemist shop or get a prescription from your doctor.
Fallopian tubes	The two tubes between the ovaries and the uterus. Eggs travel down them once a month.
Feminine hygiene	Another name for sanitary products, i.e. pads, towels, STs, tampons. This name is often used in large shops or supermarkets.
Fertile	Able to become pregnant.

Fertilisation	When a sperm and an egg join together.
Foetus	(May also be spelt *fetus*.) An unborn baby which grows and develops in the uterus (womb).
Genitals/genitalia	The parts of the reproductive system on the outside of the body.
Labia	Sometimes called lips. These are the folds of skin that enclose the vulva between the legs. The labia majora are the outer pair and the labia minora are the inner pair.
Menarche	The time in a young woman's life when she starts her periods, i.e. has her first period.
Menopause	The time in a woman's life when the ovaries stop producing eggs and periods end.
Mucus	A slimy substance produced by the mucous glands which are found in the cervix and other parts of the body.
Nausea	Feeling sick.
Nipple	The part of a woman's breast which

sticks out. A baby sucks on the nipple to get milk.

Oestrogen — This is one of the hormones produced by women. At puberty it is needed for some of the body changes like breast growth.

Ovaries — In women there are two ovaries that produce eggs. If an egg is fertilised by a man's sperm a baby may develop. The ovaries are in the lower part of the tummy, one on either side of the uterus.

Penis — The male sexual organ. The part of a boy's or man's body that urine and sperm come out of.

Pharmacist — The person (usually wearing a white coat) in a chemist's shop (pharmacy) in charge of selling medicines and making up doctors' prescriptions. Can also give lots of useful advice.

Polycystic ovary syndrome — A problem with hormones that can cause weight gain and hairiness.

Progesterone — One of the female hormones that helps to get the uterus ready each month in case a foetus needs to grow and develop there.

Prostaglandins — Female hormones which act on the

	uterus to help it squeeze out the dead cells and blood that make up a period.
Puberty	The body changes that take place as a child develops into an adult. Starting your periods (menarche) is one of these changes.
Pubic area	The pubic area is the bit between your legs at the bottom of your tummy.
Pubic hair	The hair which grows between your legs as you develop into an adult.
Reproductive organs	The parts of the body involved in producing a baby. In girls, these are the ovaries, Fallopian tubes, uterus, cervix, vagina and vulva.
Sanitary product	Something you use to soak up the blood from your period. Towels, pads, STs, tampons, etc.
Scrotum	The sac (or bag) of skin which contains a male's testes. It hangs between the legs behind the penis.
Semen (or seminal fluid)	The liquid containing sperm which comes out of a penis.
Sperm	The male sex cells which can join with a female egg to form a baby. Sperm are made in the testes.

Stools	Another name for poo, number twos, faeces.
Testes	The plural of testis (one testis; two testes).
Testis	Also called "testicles", "bollocks" and "balls". In males there are two testes which produce sperm. Each testis is enclosed in the scrotum which hangs behind the penis.
Toxic shock syndrome (TSS)	A life-threatening illness caused by blood-poisoning. Can happen if a tampon is left in for too long.
Urethra	The narrow tube which urine passes through from the bladder. It opens between your legs where the urine (pee) comes out.
Urine	Pee or wee. Urine is made by the kidneys and is then stored in your bladder until you go to the lavatory. Urine is made up mainly of things that your body needs to get rid of. It is usually a pale yellow colour.
Uterus	An upside-down-pear-shaped organ in the lower part of the tummy. This is where a baby grows. It is also where the blood comes from during a period.

Vagina — One of the three openings between a girl's legs. It is a muscular tube connecting the uterus and cervix to the outside.

Vaginal discharge — Fluid which comes out of the vagina. It is usually pale creamy colour, and not smelly or itchy.

Vomiting — Being sick, throwing up.

Vulva — The name given to the outside part of the female sexual organs. It includes the openings of the vagina and urethra.

Womb — Another name for the uterus.

Index